A History of

ST. RITA PARISH

St. Rita Parish Centennial Committee

THE
History
PRESS

Published by The History Press
Charleston, SC
www.historypress.com

Opposite: St. Rita of Cascia. *Centennial History Subcommittee.*

Upper-left front cover: St. Rita School dedication, September 1952. *St. Rita Parish Archives. Upper-right front cover*: St. Rita schoolgirls entering church, circa 1950s. *St. Rita Parish Archives. Lower front cover*: St. Rita Church front façade. *Dori Rutherford.* Back cover: Father Daniel Gee, St. Rita pastor, presiding at a Palm Sunday procession, April 2014. *Arlington Catholic Herald.*

First published 2024

Manufactured in the United States

ISBN 9781467156752

Library of Congress Control Number: 2024937562

To our patroness,
St. Rita of Cascia,

And the faithful of St. Rita,
over the course of a century.

Ad Majorem Dei Gloriam—
To the Greater Glory of God

CONTENTS

Foreword by Bishop Michael F. Burbidge   7
Introduction by Father Christopher P. Christensen   9

The Years Before the Parish   11
The Early Years, 1924–1947   27
The Monsignor Gallagher Years, 1947–1967   39
A Time of Change, 1967–1986   55

*Interlude. St. Rita: La Comunidad de Hispanohablantes
(The Spanish-Speaking Community)*   73

Further Growth, 1986–2000   79
Entering the New Millennium, 2000–2010   94
St. Rita Today and Tomorrow, 2010–Present   108

Appendix A. Sisters of St. Joseph Who Served at St. Rita School,
Parish, and Convent and St. Rita School Principals   131
Appendix B. A Guide to St. Rita Church: A Catechism in Stone
and Glass   139
Acknowledgements   157
About the Contributors   159

FOREWORD

To the Faithful of Saint Rita Parish

Dear Brothers and Sisters in Christ,

I extend my congratulations to you on the occasion of the 100th anniversary of Saint Rita Parish. I join you in thanking our Lord for the many blessings he has given and in praying for his continued protection and guidance.

This joyous occasion is a beautiful way to experience the richness and vibrancy of your parish, and it is my hope that the pages of this book will convey the unique history of Saint Rita Parish in the Diocese of Arlington. I am grateful to your pastor, Father Christopher Christensen, and all the priests who have served at Saint Rita Parish for their priestly ministry and example.

Please be assured of my continued prayers for you. Through the intercession of Saint Rita, may our Lord Jesus bless you, and may his Holy Spirit lead and guide the faithful of this parish community.

Sincerely in Christ,

Most Reverend Michael F. Burbidge
Bishop of Arlington

INTRODUCTION

One hundred years is not a long time in the history of the Catholic Church, not to mention the world. But the twentieth century was full of marvel and discovery, taking us from dreams about flying to putting a man on the Moon. St. Rita Catholic Church saw most of that century, beginning small but today bustling and thriving with life and activity.

As with all the works of the Church, the story of St. Rita is a story of grace. After only three years serving as pastor, it is very clear to me that there is something special about this parish. Every parish is meant to be a place to which people come not just for a fill-up or tune-up, as if the parish were just a sacramental gas station, but rather a hub for the community of believers throughout their lives. At St. Rita, the love of God and neighbor is palpable, and the necessity of the Church (the Sacraments, grace, and other members of the Body of Christ) in that enterprise is well understood.

St. Rita is full of parishioners of all ages, some of whom are lifelong members and others more recent arrivals. I often like to joke with parishioners that our Sunday Masses are some of the loudest Masses I have ever been to because there are so many children! These families are a great blessing to our parish, and it is a privilege to impart the Catholic faith to those who are the future of the Church. They, along with the other members of the parish, help create the vibrant community that our parishioners love so much.

Our large Spanish-speaking population adds another element of diversity to the parish. The presence of immigrants from across Central America and elsewhere helps to remind us that the salvation of souls is our first responsibility. We are always seeking ways to live out with them and for them the mysteries of our salvation.

A more recent addition to an already diverse and thriving parish are those who attend the Traditional Latin Mass. The presence of this Mass at St. Rita keeps us profoundly connected to the tradition of Holy Mother Church's liturgy and enriches our understanding of the Holy Mass itself.

I pray that as you read through this brief history of St. Rita Catholic Church, you will see how God has blessed this church and this community. I pray also that you will be strengthened in your own faith so that you, along with this parish, will be a faithful witness to Christ in the world.

In Christ,
REVEREND CHRISTOPHER CHRISTENSEN
Pastor

THE YEARS BEFORE THE PARISH

*T*he story of St. Rita Parish officially begins in 1924, but the history of the Catholic faith in Virginia and in the parish's city of Alexandria long predates that year. Centuries before the establishment of either St. Rita Mission or Parish, the Catholic Church in Virginia developed largely from European forebears, who brought their religions, ambitions, hopes, and conflicts along with them. The early European colonists in Virginia were largely Protestant, with a few Catholics and other minority religions.

THE FIRST VIRGINIA CATHOLIC COLONISTS

The English arrived at Jamestown in 1607, bringing the Anglican Church and English laws. The second Virginia Company charter in 1609 forbade anyone believing in the "superstitions of the Church of Rome" from gaining passage to the New World unless he took the oath of supremacy of the king of England over the pope. However, archaeological evidence suggests that there were Catholics in Jamestown who may have practiced their faith secretly.

Some Catholics did settle in Virginia, including George Calvert, Lord Baltimore, who soon established the Maryland colony, and the prominent

Brent family of Stafford County. The growth of Maryland, with its early principles of religious toleration, brought English Jesuits and other Catholics, some of whom entered Virginia. During the following century, Jesuit and Franciscan missionaries in Maryland visited Virginia to minister to the few Catholics there. Nevertheless, the Catholic religion remained illegal, and there were various episodes of suppression and persecution. In 1745, for example, Virginia's lieutenant governor ordered the people "to be diligent in apprehending and bringing to Justice the said Romish priests, or any of them, so that they may be prosecuted according to law."

Crucifixes such as this one found at Jamestown suggest that Catholics were among the first settlers. *Historic Jamestowne.*

THE AMERICAN REVOLUTION BRINGS RELIGIOUS FREEDOM TO VIRGINIA—AND TO ALEXANDRIA

The American Revolution changed the laws concerning Catholics in Virginia. The ideals of the nation's founding fathers and the alliance of the Patriots with Catholic France made Virginia a more hospitable place for the Catholics living here, who, by the estimation of Father John Carroll, who ministered to them, numbered around two hundred. George Washington began to quell anti-Catholic tactics among his troops when he forbade them from burning an effigy of the pope on Guy Fawkes Day.

In 1775, George Mason of Fairfax County drafted the Virginia Declaration of Rights, which guaranteed religious toleration "according to the dictates of conscience," and he took steps to end the favors extended to the Anglican Church. James Madison replaced "toleration" with the stronger language of the equal entitlement of all to the "free exercise of religion according to the dictates of conscience," but he, too, stopped short of disestablishing the Anglican Church. In 1777, Thomas Jefferson drafted the Virginia Statute for Religious Freedom, forbidding compulsory attendance at any place of worship and preventing the government from collecting taxes to support any religious institution. It was finally passed into law in 1786.

A few years before Jefferson's law was passed, in 1781, John Fitzgerald, a prominent Catholic merchant in Alexandria, witnessed the first public Mass

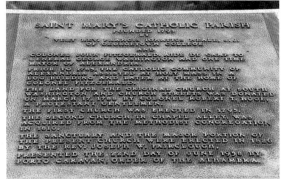

Left: George Mason's contributions to religious liberty in Virginia and the nation are often overlooked. *1811 painting by Dominic Boudet after a portrait of 1750 by John Hesselius.*

Right: A plaque at the Basilica of St. Mary's tells of the contributions of John Fitzgerald to the founding of Virginia's first Catholic parish. *From the* Arlington Catholic Herald.

in the city when a chaplain in the French army celebrated Mass for the troops. Fitzgerald had since 1769 attended Masses offered by the Jesuits of Georgetown in private homes. During the Revolutionary War, Fitzgerald had served as secretary and aide-de-camp to George Washington and, after the war, as Alexandria's mayor. In 1788, Fitzgerald invited Washington with some other dignitaries to his home to offer support for the ratification of the U.S. Constitution. He took advantage of the occasion to ask the assistance of those present in building Virginia's first Catholic church. He received money from Washington and land from two other guests for the building of St. Mary Church, the predecessor of the Basilica of St. Mary, which opened its doors in 1795 as a mission church of Trinity Church in Georgetown. St. Mary was part of the newly founded diocese of Baltimore, whose first bishop was Father John Carroll.

Although the pope established the Diocese of Richmond in 1820, Alexandria remained within the Diocese of Baltimore throughout the early nineteenth century. Even in 1847, when Alexandria officially was returned to Virginia, it remained within that diocese. It was not until 1858 that the third bishop of Richmond, John McGill, inherited Alexandria. But St. Mary was still administered by the Jesuits of Georgetown, and Bishop McGill was content to leave the area to them, busy as he was establishing new churches.

Catholic Immigration to Alexandria

Over the course of the nineteenth century, a wide range of Europeans came to Alexandria. Some came from Germany and the old Austro-Hungarian empire. Millions of Irish fled their native land during the potato famine of the 1840s and 1850s, and many of them settled in Alexandria, where they first worked as unskilled laborers. Around 1880, Italian immigrants began coming as well, as Alexandria industrialized and grew into a manufacturing center. Many of them came to work on the railroad at Alexandria's Potomac Yard, the largest railcar classification yard on the East Coast (perhaps in the United States). Their work there sometimes provoked hostility from locals.

Workers moved to Alexandria's newly developing "trolley suburbs," Del Ray, Abington, and St. Elmo. The closest Mass for the few Catholic workers and their families in the area was four miles away. There was a trolley service to St. Mary (in today's Old Town Alexandria), to Holy Trinity (in Georgetown), and to St. James (in Falls Church, Virginia), but the streetcars

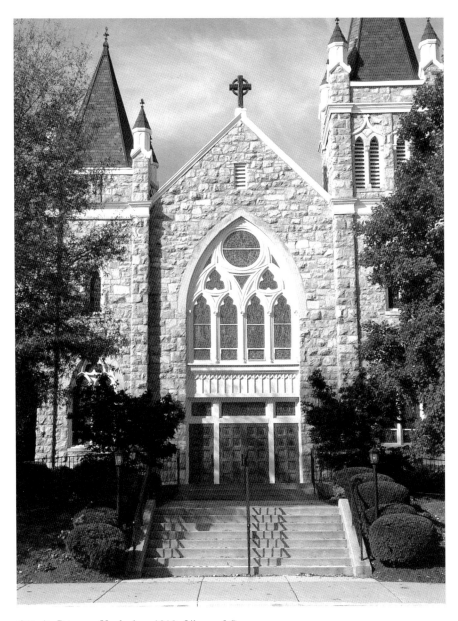

Opposite: Potomac Yard, circa 1919. *Library of Congress.*

Above: Built in 1902, St. James in Falls Church was an option for Mass. *St. James Catholic Church, Falls Church, Virginia.*

Bishop Van de Vyver, who appointed Father Henry Cutler as the first resident pastor of St. Mary's. *Diocese of Richmond.*

ran infrequently on Sundays. Almost as soon as they settled in their new home, the Catholic residents started dreaming of a church of their own. By 1890, a small chapel had been built on Peyton Avenue, but it does not seem that Mass was ever held there.

There was an immediate need for the Catholic residents—catechesis for their children. Bishop Augustine Van de Vyver, the sixth bishop of Richmond, directed that religious instruction of children in public schools in the diocese be provided by parishes outside of school hours. Many Del Ray Catholic families had their children in public school, although some attended Alexandria's Catholic schools, including the parochial schools at St. Mary and St. James, the private St. Mary's Academy for girls, and the Xaverian Brothers' School for boys. But these schools were still far away from the suburban areas and still required trolleys, whose fares, even at just a few cents a day each way, added up for the largely working-class Catholic families.

Some of the local Catholic girls took the bus to St. Mary's Academy in Alexandria. *Library of Congress.*

The Xaverian Brothers School opened in 1919 for boys. *Office of Historic Alexandria.*

213 East Custis Street, former site of Tony Guiffre's cobbler shop. *Centennial History Subcommittee.*

In 1912 the Alexandria Ladies Seminarian Society, a group of local Catholic women, opened a Sunday school in Del Ray "to care for the religious education of young children attending the district school, and who from distance or other causes could not attend the regular Sunday School at St. Mary on Sunday mornings." They secured a space for the Sunday school on East Custis Avenue: the shop of cobbler Gaetano Antonio (Tony) Guiffre, a St. Mary parishioner. Tony Guiffre would eventually go on to become a major beer distributor in the area when Prohibition ended.

A committee of mothers and sisters of the children attending the cobbler shop Sunday school organized to raise money to buy the catechisms and pay rent for the shop. Mary Conlon, who had two school-aged children at the time, was the president of the committee. Her eldest daughter, Mary, was the financial secretary. Inspired by a talk they had heard at St. Mary about the "patron saint of impossible causes," they named their Sunday school for St. Rita and called themselves the St. Rita's Ladies Society. Catechesis at the cobbler shop began in October 1912, with some fifty-six children and many of their parents attending. On November 14, the Ladies raised funds by sponsoring a progressive euchre tournament at the Young Men's Sodality (St. Mary) Lyceum. The following month, the *Evening Star* advertised a supper to benefit the Sunday school.

St. Rita of Cascia

Given that she was the inspiration for those dedicated women and is now the parish patroness, a word about St. Rita is in order. She was born in 1381 (some sources say alternatively in 1386) at Rocca Porena in the Diocese of Spoleto in present-day Italy, and her great desire had been to be a nun. However, she obeyed her parents and married a rather cruel-hearted man at a young age. For eighteen years, she was a model wife and mother, and as a result of her efforts, her husband did become kinder and more congenial. Nonetheless, he was murdered due to a long-standing family feud. She implored her sons not to seek revenge but rather to make peace, and they later died before they could commit the grievous sin of murder. She then, as a widow, sought admission to the Augustinian convent in Cascia and, as a condition of entry, reconciled the families of the feud that led to her husband's death—a seemingly insurmountable challenge, which, once she overcame it, may have been one reason that she was designated the saint of impossible causes. As a nun, she became renowned for her piety and charity, as well as for the stigmata on her forehead that she received at the age of sixty—in her case, a wound seemingly caused by one of the thorns that encircled Christ's head. She died in 1457 and was ultimately canonized in 1900 by Pope Leo XIII.

St. Rita of Cascia, surrounded by roses. *Mary Pat Schlickenmaier.*

The First Mass

In June 1913, Mrs. Henry Kraemer hosted a dinner at her home with Father Henry Cutler to secure his permission to have Mass said in the Sunday school. Father Cutler, appointed by Bishop Van de Vyver as the first resident pastor of St. Mary, had already thought about the possibility of a mission

The Conlon family home on Myrtle (now Mosby) Street. *Centennial History Subcommittee.*

church in the suburbs. The next month, the *Washington Herald* published the following announcement: "Mass will be celebrated at 9 o'clock tomorrow morning at St. Rita's Sunday school building, Del Ray, Alexandria County. It is announced that it will be celebrated at that hour every Sunday until further notice."

On July 16, 1913, Father James Van Ingelgem of St. James celebrated the first Mass at St. Rita Sunday School. St. Rita thereafter became a mission church of St. Mary, and assistant priests from St. Mary celebrated Mass in the cobbler's shop until the crowds grew so big that people were kneeling in the street.

When the weather began to get colder in October, St. Rita mission "church" moved Masses to the Mount Ida summer home of George Beuchert. The next summer, Masses were moved to the Mount Ida homes of Peter Conlon and William Becker. By this time, the new church was under construction nearby, and soon its basement would be complete and able to accommodate Mass.

The First Church

The local Catholics formed three committees to oversee the building and financing of this first St. Rita Church. Peter Conlon chaired the building committee of Father Cutler, George Beuchert, Henry Kraemer, and August Beyler. They selected an architect, Leon Clarke, to draw up plans for the proposed building. In January 1914, they met with Bishop Denis O'Connell, who had succeeded Bishop Van de Vyver in 1912. The St. Rita's Ladies Society had already apprised the bishop of the plans for a church, the number of Catholics it would potentially serve (175), and the donation by James Groves of two lots of land for the purpose.

In 1908, Groves bought the century-old Mount Ida house on Russell Road and 150 acres of land surrounding it from heirs of the Alexander family, after whom the city was named. Groves moved into the house, established the Mount Ida Real Estate Company, and sold plots of land to prospective homeowners. Bishop O'Connell was able to exchange the plots originally donated by Groves for two more suitable plots on Maple (now Hickory) Street with a view of the Potomac. In February, the building committee awarded the building contract to Julien D. Knight of Alexandria. One month later, on March 21, 1914, the builders broke ground.

In the meantime, a second committee of the future parish calling itself the Ladies Missionary Society set up an office in Washington at 700 10th Street, NW. Mary Barbour was the president of the society, and Agnes Graumann was its secretary. They raised funds for the project outside of the parish and were responsible for securing the bulk of the financing. The third committee, the St. Rita's Ladies Society, raised funds within the parish, establishing at the same time some of the activities that would become the life of the fledgling parish: a chicken dinner, an oyster supper, a three-day bazaar, and a Valentine's Day masked ball. In the face of various setbacks, including the collapse of the back wall of the church and the unexpected death of a promised donor, the committee members prayed novenas to St. Rita and redoubled their efforts.

On May 17, 1914, the cornerstone was laid for the new church, with the customary box containing coins and papers placed inside. Bishop O'Connell was in Rome at the time, so Patrick Conlon invited the apostolic delegate, Archbishop Giovanni Bonzano, to lay the stone and give a papal blessing. The ceremonies were held "under the auspices of" the Ancient Order of Hibernians (AOH), Alexandria Division, and both the national president of the AOH James Regan and the national president of the

Right: Bishop Denis J. O'Connell, who approved the plans to build the first St. Rita Church. *Diocese of Richmond.*

Below: The cornerstone of the original church was preserved when the church was dismantled. *Eamonn Greiner.*

Ladies Auxiliary of the AOH were invited to speak. Conlon also invited the Washington members of the Holy Name Society to attend, wearing their identifying pins. Father William Kerby of Catholic University in Washington gave the principal address, exhorting the men and women of St. Rita to "[b]e glad this center of power is added to your community for it makes it easier to fight your battles."

DEDICATION OF THE CHURCH

The community only had to wait until October before the construction of the church was complete. This small church, part brick and part concrete block, was built on a budget, but it still inspired the faithful with its simple

The original St. Rita church on Maple (now Hickory) Street. *St. Rita Parish Archives.*

The congregation of Engleside Baptist dismantled the old church in 1954 and moved it brick by brick to its current location. *Wikimedia Commons.*

beauty. After the newer, larger St. Rita Church was built in 1949, the older church was taken down brick by brick and reassembled at its new location at 8428 Highland Lane in Alexandria, where it stands today, albeit with modifications, as the Engleside Baptist Church.

At 10:30 a.m. on Sunday, October 18, 1914, Bishop O'Connell formally dedicated the church on Maple Street to St. Rita. Father Cutler offered the first Mass in the new church. William Becker supervised the altar servers, and the St. Rita choir, augmented by members of St. Mary choir, provided the music. Fittingly, Father Thomas Delihant of Loyola College gave a sermon on "The Promised Land."

Life in the Mission Church, 1914–1924

The month after its opening, the church saw its first baptism. The baby girl born to Henry Kraemer and his wife was named Rita. Camille De Lane, who played the pump organ in the new church, had the honor of playing at the first wedding on July 15, 1915: that of her own mother to L.E. Tull of Washington, D.C. Peter Conlon Jr. married Helen Beall in June 1918, and in 1919, they named and baptized their daughter, also Rita.

Father Cutler died in August 1915, and Father Louis Smet became pastor of St. Mary and therefore responsible for the St. Rita Mission. Under his leadership, grace continued to flow through the Sacraments

First Communicants, May 26, 1918. *St. Rita Parish Archives.*

Camille De Lane, first organist of the church. *St. Rita Parish Archives.*

and devotional practices. Bishop O'Connell came to the church on December 13, 1915, to confirm twenty-one children and seven adults. In May 1917, one month after the United States entered World War I, a visiting priest led Vespers and gave a talk at the commencement of a novena to St. Rita. St. Mary priests also came to the church for her feast day's celebration on May 22.

The *Alexandria Gazette* tells a story of the devotion and bravery of an early St. Rita parishioner. It was customary for the priests who came to St. Rita's on Sundays to leave the chalice, paten, and ciborium at the nearby home of William Becker during the week for safekeeping, as there was not a suitable place for them in the church. William Becker was the leader of the altar servers and may have acted as the church's first sacristan. During the night of September 1, 1916, Mr. Becker woke up to find that his house was on fire. After getting his family out of the house, Mr. Becker risked life and limb to return inside to save the sacred vessels, although his money and possessions went up in smoke.

During World War I, from 1917 to 1918, the U.S. Army stationed a camp of soldiers at the old St. Asaph's racetrack nearby. St. Rita opened its church hall for recreation for the soldiers every evening, and it provided books and writing materials to the soldiers in the hall free of charge. St. Rita faithful had other opportunities to practice charity, for instance, toward the so-called rail riders who would periodically come into the neighborhood to beg for food. Longtime parishioner Patricia Downey McArtor recalled that these were young men, not frightening, "who would just walk up the street… and knock on the door…and want to know if you had any extra food or a sandwich or something like that."

The St. Rita Ladies Society offered the social and cultural events that were necessary to the life of the parish. Strawberry festivals, chicken dinners, lawn fetes, and bazaars in the church hall provided opportunities for families to practice their faith together in the activities of daily life. Father Smet introduced to the community both the League of the Sacred Heart, which

William Becker (*front center*) with Father Daly, Leo Parsons, and altar servers (1916). *St. Rita Parish Archives.*

had been successful in Belgium in encouraging men to religious involvement, and the Blessed Virgin Mary Sodality, which became the new name of the St. Rita Ladies Society. In 1921, the newspaper announced that the St. Rita Assembly, a Catholic fraternity, would be meeting for the first time in its new headquarters on August 26.

A Parish Is Established

By 1924, St. Rita had become large and active enough to make it considerably challenging to run as simply a mission. Father Smet thus petitioned Bishop O'Connell to appoint a resident pastor for St. Rita and thereby make it an independent parish. The bishop granted the petition, and in May 1924, Father Leonard J. Koster was installed at St. Rita as its first resident pastor. Later that year, on September 21, 1924, St. Rita became a parish. The journey had been remarkable. The early faithful of St. Rita had been, in their own way, colonists just as the settlers in Virginia had been centuries before. As Father Kerby noted when the cornerstone of the first St. Rita Church was laid, "When you build a new church you become colonizers to carry the message of Christ. I compliment you for having started a new colony for the supernatural."

THE EARLY YEARS, 1924–1947

A New Parish

Father (later Monsignor) Leonard Koster. *St. Rita Parish Archives.*

In the years after the First World War, streetcar suburbs like Mount Ida and Potomac saw a period of steady growth. The dozen or so families who first sought to bring the Holy Sacrifice of the Mass closer to their homes had grown to a community with more than 370 members in its first decade as a mission within Saint Mary Parish. In recognition of these fruits that had sprung forth from such humble beginnings, the little brick church was named as a parish on September 21, 1924, and Bishop Denis O'Connell installed Father Leonard Koster as St. Rita's first pastor.

Father Koster was a native of Richmond, where he attended Sacred Heart School and Benedictine High School. His formation for the priesthood began with minor seminary at St. Charles College in Catonsville, Maryland, as was a common practice in that time. His education continued at Belmont Abbey in North Carolina, where he was ordained in 1919. Over the next five years, he served parishes in Richmond, Staunton, and Newport News.

As a new pastor at a new parish, Father Koster had considerable assistance in ministering to his flock. The Dominican Sisters of St. Dominic Parish in Washington, D.C., supervised the Sunday school, and Capuchin Father Felix Kirsch preached at Mass for the first time that October. The Capuchins began preaching regularly at Mass in the fall of 1927, a role that they continued up to the 1970s. With the help of the National Council of Catholic Women, the Mission Helpers of the Sacred Heart from Baltimore were invited to supervise First Communion preparation and offer vacation religion school, which was something of a novelty in the region.

Father Koster's missionary zeal was matched by his business acumen, seemingly tireless energy, and persuasive determination. As was then the custom, he would make annual rounds to the home of each family, and his parishioners gave him the nickname "the Flying Parson" for the apparent omnipresence of his speeding automobile as he traveled to and fro within

Father Koster with mission helpers. *St. Rita Parish Archives.*

the parish bounds. In one instance, he arranged for five roasted turkeys to be transported from the Raleigh Hotel in Washington to feed the guests at a fundraiser, doubtlessly astounding those in attendance when he arrived to carve the birds despite the lack of any kitchen in the parish hall.

Growth and Life of the Community

The new parish celebrated its first baptism with the twins Norbert and Eugene Graumann. On January 25, 1925, Father Koster celebrated the Sacrament of Matrimony for the first time as pastor, blessing the union of

Harry Sullivan and Ethel Botts. In the next decade, interdenominational weddings outnumbered those between Catholic spouses by two to one. It is perhaps fitting that women led the effort to build the little brick church and also built up the Universal Church by bringing many souls into the parish through their marriages—a pattern often observed in the history of the Church.

During these early years, the laity began organizing new programs for the community, such as the drama club started by Mary Conlon in 1925. The Ladies' Society, which had been so instrumental in the formation of St. Rita, was known as the Sanctuary Society at the time of St. Rita's elevation to the level of parish and boasted 100 percent registration of the women on the parish rolls. Their frequent parties and suppers raised the much-needed funds for the maintenance of the church and the Sunday school.

The Holy Name Society predated St. Rita's designation as a parish but was formally chartered in 1925, with Peter Conlon Sr. as its first chapter president. The society's central mission dates to the fifteenth century when Didacus of Victoria created a rule for governing a society to uphold the Second Commandment ("Thou shalt not take the Name of the Lord thy God in vain") by promoting reverence for the Sacred Names of God and Jesus Christ. The rule was approved by Pope Pius IV in 1564, and the society was placed under the direction of the Dominican Order by his successor, Pope St. Pius V, in 1571.

In the early days of St. Rita Parish, the Holy Name Society participated in monthly nocturnal adoration and annual Lenten retreats. The men of the parish sponsored annual dances and hosted Communion breakfasts featuring notable clergy, politicians, academics, and athletes as special guest speakers over the years. Notwithstanding the pious mission of the society, members interviewed in the 1970s would recall that local sports figures tended to draw the strongest attendance.

Depression and the New Deal

The Great Depression brought many changes and challenges to St. Rita Parish. As a sign of more austere times, the drama club disbanded in 1929. In 1930, the City of Alexandria annexed most of Arlington County south of Four Mile Run. As part of the annexation, many streets were renamed, and the church found itself adorning Hickory Street instead of Walnut Street. In

Streetcar crossing Four Mile Run Causeway. *Town of Potomac Historical Association.*

1932, the streetcar running on Washington Avenue—now Commonwealth Avenue—that connected Mount Ida to downtown Alexandria and Washington ceased operations. The ten-cent fare was an unaffordable luxury when many could not spare a dime to buy a meal.

The working-class parishioners of St. Rita acutely felt the privations of the era. Census rolls for 1930 show that the railroads were the main employer in Mount Ida, and their business was hit hard by the economic crisis. However, those who lived through the toughest years would later recall that most of the family breadwinners remained employed. Although there was never extra money, the Sanctuary Society managed to collect steady donations for upkeep of the church—a credit to the intercession of our patroness and Father Koster's frugality.

Despite the difficult times, the 1930s also saw a flourishing of parish life. Families pulled together to assist those in need and ensure that all would at least be clothed and fed. In an interview given in the 1970s, Father Koster described it as a very tight-knit community. The St. Rita Athletic Association was also founded in the 1930s and sponsored high school–age teams for baseball, football, and basketball for the boys and basketball and tennis for the girls. In 1934, the Sanctuary Society began hosting bingo nights.

St. Rita girls' basketball team in 1930s. *St. Rita Parish Archives.*

At the beginning of the 1930s, Mount Ida and Potomac were small towns with a rural character, and much of the surrounding area was woodlands and farms. Several stone quarries were located in the hills overlooking the Washington and Old Dominion Railroad. Census records show farm laborers and railroad machinists living alongside grocers and carpenters as well as government typists and clerks. Although linked to the capital and the region by numerous railroads, the St. Rita community was in many ways a small, sleepy southern town.

The election of President Franklin D. Roosevelt in 1932 brought enormous changes to the nation and to the region. The population of Alexandria began to increase significantly with the New Deal expansion of the federal government. Between 1927 and 1936, several new subdivisions appear on contemporary aerial photos. In 1937, Presidential Gardens (now Presidential Greens) was one of the first apartment complexes to be built in the area. The site directly across the street from the present church was originally the baseball field for a semi-professional Negro League team, the Hume Springs Nine. Appropriately for a housing development in the New Deal era, the columns for the portico of the Washington building facing Mount Vernon Avenue were taken from the stage for Roosevelt's second inauguration.

Inauguration of Franklin D. Roosevelt in 1933. *Library of Congress.*

The construction boom brought major demographic changes to the community and to St. Rita Parish. The area north of the railroad tracks was mostly marshy ground and had been thinly settled, predominantly by African Americans, but was now being built up to provide much-needed housing for an expanding federal workforce. Between 1930 and 1936, the number of parishioners at St. Rita had increased by 50 percent. By 1940, as the Second World War was raging overseas and the United States was ramping up wartime production to assist our allies, the congregation had more than doubled.

A NEW MISSION

The original parish boundaries were entirely within Arlington County and extended to the border of St. Charles Parish to the north. Within those limits, the area now known as Crystal City was the site of several brickworks that supplied materials for numerous structures across the river, including the Willard Hotel. In 1903, a trade journal listed the output of five factories in what was then known as "Brick Haven" as 100 million bricks per year. It's possible that these factories also supplied the bricks for the original St. Rita Church on Hickory Street. One factory, the New Washington Brick Company, owned Abingdon, formerly the home of the Custis family. By

Aerial photo of
Memorial Bridge and
George Washington
Parkway. *Arlington County
Library*.

1924, the estate had fallen into disrepair and was sold to the Richmond, Fredericksburg, and Potomac Railroad so it could expand Potomac Yard.

With all this industrial activity in the 1920s, the surrounding landscape was carved up by steam shovels to harvest the Virginia clay, and clouds of black smoke from the brick furnaces and steam locomotives filled the sky. The dynamic energy and growth of the surrounding community contributed to the growth of St. Rita Parish. Because of the extent of the boundaries and the rapid growth of the region, a new mission was founded to serve the Aurora Highlands community and was named in honor of Saint Ann.

Just as many of the first Masses in the Mount Ida community were held in private homes, the first Mass in Aurora Highlands was offered by Father Koster in the Lash family home on September 11, 1927. Father Koster had a full schedule of Masses, so the Capuchin fathers assisted with Masses at both locations. The Lash home soon proved inadequate, as weekly Mass attendance surpassed sixty people. Beginning in 1928, Mass was offered in the fire hall at 23rd and Eads Streets until a suitable chapel could be built. Bishop Andrew Brennan had already begun acquiring land in 1927, but it would take another decade to raise the necessary funds for construction.

Despite the lack of funds, the community continued to grow. The Memorial Bridge was completed in 1932, and the George Washington Memorial Parkway was also built—largely following the right-of-way of the defunct streetcar line—providing an additional link to the capital. That same year, the various communities within Arlington County coordinated to rename all the streets under a unified numeric and alphabetic scheme to assist the post office with the increased volume of mail. During the 1930s, the community became much more aligned with the federal government, which became the primary employer.

Although the growing community badly needed a church of its own, the difficulty of raising funds during the Great Depression was insurmountable, and construction for the new mission church would not begin until 1939. Ground was broken that summer, and the basement of a new church at 23rd and Hayes Streets was consecrated by Father Thomas Rankin, Vicar Forane for Northern Virginia, on November 19, 1939, under the patronage of Our Lady of Lourdes. However, even as this church was being completed, it was already becoming evident that it would not be large enough to meet the needs of the faithful.

A Nation at War

To meet the growing needs of St. Rita Parish, Father Thomas Finnegan was appointed as the first associate pastor in 1939, serving until 1942. At the outbreak of the Second World War, many of the parishioners of St. Rita were first-generation immigrants from Germany and Italy, which were now our enemies, or from neutral Ireland, but this did not diminish their patriotic zeal to serve their adopted country. Conscription began in 1940, and by the end of the war, nearly every family in the parish was represented in the blue star honor roll at the back of the church. This cosmopolitan combination of cultures would soon be joined by a new wave of arrivals with the massive build-up of military personnel and defensive preparations to secure the nation's capital.

For many years, nearby Hoover Airfield had a deplorable safety record. Smokestacks of the brickworks, landfills (often on fire), power lines, and radio towers obstructed landings and impaired visibility. A busy road crossed the main runway, causing repeated clashes between Arlington County and the airport that eventually required Congressional intervention. The airport was widely criticized as a national disgrace and a menace to aviators and passengers alike. After many years of lobbying by aviation advocates, including Amelia Earhart, President Roosevelt appealed to Congress for the authority to construct a modern facility. After securing this legislation, National Airport opened on June 16, 1941.

The War Department then purchased the old airport site, and construction on the Pentagon began on September 11, just months before the attack on Pearl Harbor. When it was completed in 1943, the Pentagon was by far the world's largest office building and remained so until 2023. More than fifteen thousand architects, engineers, and tradesmen worked around the clock to complete this mega-project, but military planners also had to account for the enormous logistical challenge of transporting the expected thirty thousand daily commuters to the site. The Pentagon was designed from the start as a transportation hub, and the Shirley Highway also started construction in 1941. Indeed, the need for office space was so acute that employees began to move in before the building was finished.

These back-to-back projects brought a literal army of workers— construction was led by the Army Corps of Engineers—within the parish boundaries. Despite large tracts of housing being built during the war, many of these new workers had to live in dormitories or trailer homes due to the shortage of housing. Likewise, the original St. Rita church and the Lourdes Chapel were already proving inadequate. Faced with this wartime influx of new parishioners, Father Koster looked for alternative venues to celebrate Sunday Mass as an emergency measure. Initially, Mass was offered at the Palm Theater, but this also proved too small; by 1942, a noon Mass was being offered weekly at the larger Vernon Theater. Coincidentally, in 1940, Father Koster began acquiring land from the Beall and Conlon families precisely because it was centrally located within the original parish boundaries. This property across Mount Vernon Avenue from the Vernon Theater later became the site of the present church.

The use of a movie theater for celebrating Mass is something of a historical irony, as the 1930s had seen a spirited public debate over morality and chastity—or lack thereof—as portrayed by Hollywood, with the Catholic Church exerting considerable public influence. The National Legion of Decency was founded in 1933 by Archbishop John McNicholas to encourage Catholics to boycott indecent films. Simultaneously, Hollywood adopted the Motion Picture Production Code under William Hays. However Father Koster may have personally felt about the movies, the dramatic growth of his parish left him with no other options and the Vernon Theater provided a pragmatic short-term solution. In 1943, Father Koster also began acquiring land in Aurora Highlands for a larger church for the Lourdes mission.

The war years also saw changes in the clergy at St. Rita. Father Finnegan was transferred to the Cathedral of the Sacred Heart in Richmond and would eventually be appointed to Holy Cross Parish in Lynchburg, where he also served as a chaplain for the Newman Center at Randolph-Macon Women's College. Father William McGonigle was appointed as assistant

Father McGonigle with altar boys. *St. Rita Parish Archives.*

pastor, and he would serve St. Rita for many years. On May 21, 1944, Bishop Ireton celebrated the silver jubilee of Father Koster's ordination. Father Finnegan returned from Richmond to mark the occasion, serving as deacon under the Tridentine rubrics.

After the War

Our Lady of Lourdes was raised to parish status by Bishop Peter Ireton, and Father Robert Beattie was installed as the first pastor there on June 9, 1946. Father Koster read a letter from the bishop at the installation Mass, while Monsignor Edward Stevens celebrated the Mass as Vicar Forane. The neighboring parishes of Our Lady Queen of Peace and Blessed Sacrament were elevated at the same time as a response to the unprecedented population expansion. The same year, St. Rita Parish started a fundraising drive to build a new main church. Also in 1946, the Sanctuary Society was officially chartered as the Women's Sodality, with Mrs. Mary Beall as its first president.

In its first two decades as a parish, the tiny seed that had been planted with a dozen or so ladies meeting in a cobbler's shop was now yielding fruit a hundredfold. This bountiful crop was not yet ready for the harvest when Father Koster was reassigned to neighboring St. Charles Parish in 1947, having served the nascent St. Rita Parish for its first twenty-three years. Although he had not fulfilled his desire to build a larger main church or Lourdes mission, he left St. Rita Parish with the considerable sum of $100,000 in the bank for his successor to carry on with the work he had so ably begun. Indeed, with the postwar boom, there would be much work to do.

Father Koster would serve until 1968 as pastor at St. Charles, where he was elevated to monsignor and led efforts to build a new church, convent, and school. He served on the building committee for Bishop O'Connell High School, which opened in 1957, and he founded the St. Coletta School for children with intellectual disabilities in 1959. The work he began providing specialized education for five children with Down syndrome at St. Charles continues up to the present as an ecumenical ministry that serves the Greater Washington metropolitan region. Monsignor Koster passed away on April 9, 1977, at the Little Sisters of the Poor Hospital in Richmond.

The early years of St. Rita Parish saw a remarkable transformation from a rural, small-town church with some three hundred parishioners to a rapidly expanding bedroom community with thousands of military personnel and other federal workers arriving within the space of a few years. The little brick church on Hickory Street was built with a view toward the eternal, but its builders could not have foreseen how dramatically the community would be reshaped by the larger forces of world events. The world of 1914 was in many ways closer to that of 1865 than to 1945, but through it all, the community of St. Rita continually adapted to the times while remaining true to the timeless.

THE MONSIGNOR GALLAGHER YEARS, 1947–1967

FATHER GALLAGHER ARRIVES

Father (later Monsignor) Emmett Gallagher. *St. Rita Parish Archives.*

In September 1947, Father Emmett P. Gallagher arrived at St. Rita as its second pastor. Born in 1896 in Pennsylvania, he had gone to public school and worked in the state's coal mines before entering the seminary. Ordained in 1921, he had subsequently served throughout the Diocese of Richmond before coming to St. Rita. He had proved himself to be a highly capable administrator and builder; indeed, he had overseen the construction of St. Francis Church in Staunton, Virginia. He was also known for his deep faith and boundless energy. Deacon Stephen Dixon remembers him as "amazing," as a priest who had an "aura" about him that radiated holiness.

His solicitude for the faithful knew no bounds. He made sure to visit every single parish family's home at least once annually. He was a superb, tireless fundraiser and planner. And he was not without an impish Irish sense of humor. St. Rita School alumnus Mike Fenwick recalled that on St. Patrick's Day, Father Gallagher would hand out silver dollars to all the schoolboys named Patrick and schoolgirls named Patricia! And his charity was inexhaustible. He was known to pay for school expenses out of his own pocket for any child who could not afford to go to St. Rita. As an "old school" priest, his sermons were described as "down to earth." They reflected his "high ideals, his firm principles, and his love of God." The parish was in his sure hands for twenty years.

BUILDING A NEW CHURCH

Appropriately enough, one of Father Gallagher's first tasks was the building of a new church. By 1940, with more than one thousand parishioners, Father Koster had recognized that a new, bigger church was needed. The three-acre tract on Russell Road that Father Koster had bought earlier would be the new church's site. Monies from special building fund collections taken during Mass, as well as building fund drives from 1946 to 1948, helped finance the project. Samuel J. Collins, whose story is recounted in Appendix B of this book, was the architect, and the general contractor was A.P. DiGuilian Inc.

St. Rita Church architect Samuel J. Collins. *St. Rita Parish Archives.*

Groundbreaking took place on September 8, 1948, with Father Gallagher at the shovel. Construction continued all through the rest of 1948 and nearly all of 1949. On December 18, 1949, the cornerstone was laid, blessed by Bishop Ireton. A copper box was placed inside it containing a 1924 letter from Bishop O'Connell to Father Koster that appointed him as the St. Rita pastor, as well as current issues of the *Catholic Virginian* and *Alexandria Gazette* that featured stories and pictures of the new church, a copy of the latest church bulletin, a copy of the parish's Jubilee Memorial Book (it was, after all, the parish's twenty-fifth anniversary), and, most significantly, a blessed medal of St. Rita. A solemn High Mass followed, with Father Koster serving as celebrant.

That Christmas Eve, confessions were first heard in the new church. Midnight Mass followed. Then, along with the next day's joyous Christmas Day Mass, Father Gallagher officiated at the first baptisms there. Less

Groundbreaking of the new church, September 8, 1948. *St. Rita Parish Archives.*

The building of the new church. *St. Rita Parish Archives.*

Right: Bishop Peter Ireton blesses the cornerstone, December 18, 1949. *St. Rita Parish Archives*.

Below: Inaugural Mass at the new church, December 18, 1949. *St. Rita Parish Archives*.

than a month later, on January 21, 1950, Father McGonigle presided over two weddings. The church, considered one of the diocese's true gems, is described in more detail in Appendix B.

A School Is Established

Soon after the church was built, Father Gallagher turned his sights on building a school. All his skill and energy were needed. Just half a year after the church was built, the Korean War broke out in the summer of 1950. That brought many government workers and military personnel to the area, along with their families. But while that meant a large number of Catholic school-aged children needed to be educated, the war also meant shortages of building material. Undeterred, that August, Fathers Gallagher and McGonigle began the plans for a six-room school, a school hall, and an adjoining convent that would house the religious Sisters who would make up the majority of the teachers. Those plans were soon altered, and a kindergarten was added to the concept. On December 29, 1951, ground was broken. T.J. Collins and Sons of Staunton, Virginia—the family firm of Samuel J. Collins, the church architect—designed both school and convent for a total cost of $275,000.

View of the lot of the future St. Rita School. *St. Rita Parish Archives.*

Opposite, top: Groundbreaking of the new school, December 29, 1951. *St. Rita Parish Archives.*

Opposite, bottom: Dedication of the new school, September 14, 1952. *St. Rita Parish Archives.*

Above: Opening day of school, September 15, 1952. *St. Rita Parish Archives.*

With Bishop Ireton's approval, Father Gallagher borrowed a considerable sum, and a major fund drive was overseen by parishioners Addison B. Clohosey and Marian Keating. The $60,000 fund drive amount was oversubscribed by $3,344, with the largest pledge coming from the parish's Blessed Virgin Mary Sodality—the $5,000 it donated was, in turn, paid off by subsequent rummage and bake sales and card parties.

Prior to opening, its plans had been changed yet again—it was redesigned to have nine classrooms. The school was dedicated on Sunday, September 14, 1952, with Bishop Ireton presiding and with Father J. Louis Flaherty, diocesan superintendent of Catholic schools, attending. It opened the next day. The first student body numbered 462, a full 130 more than had been pre-registered the previous spring!

THE SISTERS OF SAINT JOSEPH

The school was staffed by six Sisters of St. Joseph, along with three lay teachers. For nearly seventy years, the Sisters of St. Joseph would teach there. The order originated in seventeenth-century France. Under the patronage of St. Joseph, six women had dedicated themselves to the "practice of all spiritual and corporal works of mercy of which woman is capable." Eventually, the order came to the United States. In 1852, aided by the holy bishop of Philadelphia, St. John Neumann, they established their motherhouse in Chestnut Hill, Pennsylvania. They became renowned for their many works of mercy, which included serving as nurses on both sides during the American Civil War and as educators.

No doubt their reputation for holiness and competence is what caused the diocese to request them to staff what would be the St. Rita School, which they did with great energy and devotion. All the school principals were Sisters of St. Joseph until 1998. The Sisters served in all sorts of capacities, whether as teachers or as workers in the convent and, in the 1970s and 1990s, in roles such as parish director of religious education, CCD coordinator, or in the pastoral care ministry. As of this writing, some of the Sisters live in the order's retirement villa in Flourtown, Pennsylvania.

The Sisters of St. Joseph at St. Rita, outside the convent. *St. Rita Parish Archives.*

School Days

Soon after the school opened, enrollment surged. By the spring of 1953, with 555 students expected that fall, three more classrooms had to be added on the parking lot side of the school. Still, that did not suffice. In 1957, a six-room annex was built across from the rectory (the present-day Preschool and Parish Center) at a cost of $130,000. The enrollment peaked that year at 976 students.

Such enrollment was the result of several factors, including the influx of government and military families, especially given the proximity of the school to the Pentagon. Another factor was the post–World War II "baby boom," especially the "Catholic baby boom," of the era. Alumnus Mike Fenwick recalled that the education he received was excellent, despite the exceptionally

Sixth-grade girls, outside the school annex, 1963–64 class. *Mike Fenwick.*

Above: Sixth-grade boys, outside the annex, 1963–64 class. *Mike Fenwick.*

Opposite, top: May Procession, circa 1950s. *Mary Pat Schlickenmaier.*

Opposite, bottom: School Safety Patrol, circa 1950s. *St. Rita Parish Archive.*

large classes. Grammar and other fundamentals were drilled into the children from the outset, and they learned to read and write exceptionally well—he attributes his success to that education. Students brought in their own lunch, but milk (white or chocolate) could be bought at the school.

Outside the school walls, the children could be seen at recess playing tag, shooting marbles, and trading baseball cards. They participated in the big annual May procession in honor of the Blessed Virgin Mary. Children from the seventh and eighth grades made up the school safety patrols. Children generally received First Holy Communion in second grade and were confirmed in third.

Almost all the children walked to school, since they lived in the local area, such as the nearby Warwick Manor neighborhood. The surrounding area was a mix of relatively new military and government workers and more established local families, such as the Fannons and the Dyers. And

the area was indeed "family friendly"—school alumni recalled the five grocery stores in the area, as well as others such as Harvey's Store, where in the words of alumnus (and future parochial vicar) Father Mark Moretti, one could get "the best candy in town," which included everything from candy necklaces to wax Coke bottles filled with syrup to "sweet tarts the size of hockey pucks."

The Sisters of St. Joseph who taught at the school were themselves the stuff of legend, although when they first arrived, they had no place to live! Building material shortages meant that while the school was finished, the convent was still, in one of the Sisters' words, "just a hole in the ground." The St. Rita fathers moved to the St. Mary rectory on Duke Street, and the Sisters took up residence at the St. Rita rectory until the convent was finally completed in February 1953.

With classrooms seemingly filled to the limit, discipline provided by the Sisters inside them was strict, recalled Deacon Dixon, but the Sisters were good women who taught their young students the elements of the faith and how to treat others with respect. There was Mother Francis Patrick, who would serve as principal two separate tenures, from 1952 to 1958 and then from 1964 to 1968, and who was remembered as kind yet stern and "no-nonsense." She could, in Father Moretti's words, "control a school yard of 600 kids by sitting on the steps and clicking a 'cricket' at us." There was Sister Carmela, who could conduct a choir class while playing the piano behind her back. And fondly remembered was Sister St. Joan, who came to St. Rita because Father Gallagher wanted an art teacher to provide a "little culture." She taught painting to countless children and adults. For more than two decades, she held art classes in the convent basement and had art shows that displayed the work.

And while they were firm in old-fashioned and no-nonsense discipline, the Sisters were not averse to technology or to bringing in some fun. On certain occasions, a Sister would bring in a radio for the children to listen to World Series games or, in the early '60s, a black-and-white TV so the children could watch the lift-offs of the Mercury astronauts.

Parish Life

During the Gallagher era, parish numbers grew, and so too did all sorts of parish activities. Devotional practices flourished. In May 1949, First

Saturday devotions were inaugurated in honor of Our Lady of Fatima. Two years later, two men of the parish, Frank Fannon and Walter Muir, founded a Nocturnal Adoration Society (such adoration continues to the present on Fridays). Weeklong retreats were held for both women and men annually.

In 1946, just before Father Gallagher arrived, the ladies of the parish formed a Blessed Virgin Mary Sodality, with Mary Beall as its first prefect and Father McGonigle as its moderator. The sodality became a center of parish activity. It divided into thirteen subcommittees that covered all aspects of parish life, and it held bake and rummage sales, card parties, fashion shows, and fundraisers, as well as monthly retreats and annual Communion breakfasts. One sodality event that was particularly well known was the annual Mardi Gras party that brought parishioners to the school hall for a buffet supper and dancing. The guests were invited to bring in the previous year's palms so they could be burned for use on Ash Wednesday in a ceremony performed by one of the fathers. The sodality grew large enough that in 1956, a Senior Members group was organized for older ladies of the parish, who held their own events. Following the Second Vatican Council, it was restructured as the St. Rita Women's Club in 1967. As Father Gallagher commented about the Sodality, "By their efforts, they have contributed enormously to the welfare of our children and therefore they deserve our unstinted praise and cooperation."

Senior members of the Blessed Virgin Mary Sodality, circa 1959. *From the* Catholic Virginian.

Left: St. Rita CYO girls' basketball, circa 1961–62. *St. Rita Parish Archives.*

Below: St. Rita male choir along with organist Clara Colangelo. *St. Rita Parish Archives.*

There were numerous other activities. Beginning in November 1947, under the direction of Father McGonigle, the Catholic Youth Organization (CYO) came to St. Rita and sponsored various sporting events for the parish youth: parish teams competed in municipal leagues in basketball and baseball for boys and basketball and softball for girls. For Masses, a male choir was established in 1949 under the direction of Hugh Murtha and accompanied by organist Clara Colangelo. Later, a boys' section was added, taught by Sisters Rose Clare and William Gerard (known as the "music sisters"), which made possible three- and four-part music for some Masses. The Christian Family Movement, which stressed couples coming together to strengthen family ties and to improve the community, came to the parish in 1958, and the Confraternity of Christian Doctrine (CCD) began the following year and provided religious instruction for both elementary and high school children who did not attend the school.

Winds of Change

The 1960s began with a sense that the world was changing. John F. Kennedy, a young senator from Massachusetts, was elected the nation's first Catholic president. In the early part of the decade, there were great civil rights marches and other protests for racial equality. Pope Pius XII had died in 1958, and his successor, Pope John XXIII, convened in 1962 the Second Vatican Council, which would take place over the next three years. Its effect on the lives of Catholics worldwide would be profound. As the years progressed, tumult followed. President Kennedy was assassinated in 1963. American troops became increasingly involved in fighting in South Vietnam, a nation that, until then, had remained largely unknown.

During the early years of the decade, change at St. Rita seemed gradual, and if anything, things continued on a seemingly gentle upward pace. The convent was still filled with teaching Sisters—in fact, it had to be enlarged to accommodate thirteen. The school was still filled to capacity—the main school now had two classes per grade. Father Gallagher became Monsignor Gallagher in February 1961, although he humbly insisted that he still be referred to as "Father." He had always dreamed of having St. Rita be a tuition-free school and was able to get yearly costs down from thirty-six dollars to twenty-five dollars per family. Meanwhile, a diocesan boys' high school named after Bishop Ireton opened in Alexandria in 1964, and Monsignor Gallagher ensured that any boy from St. Rita whose parents wanted him to go there would go, even if they could not afford it—he would pay for the boy's costs from the gifts and benefactions that he had received and saved up over the years.

Yet some significant change eventually did come. By 1961, congregational singing became emphasized—it was announced from the pulpit to the congregation, "We expect you to sing." Then, on November 29, 1964, the first Sunday of Advent, English was used during certain parts of the Mass for the first time. One year later, men were permitted to serve as cantors, although that was discontinued around 1970. In 1966, a Home and School Association was founded by Monsignor Gallagher and Mother Francis Patrick, a forerunner to today's Parent-Teacher Organization.

One parishioner's story deserves special mention, that of Humbert Roque "Rocky" Versace. His father was U.S. Army colonel Humbert J. Versace, from Puerto Rico, and his mother, Marie Teresa, was a novelist and poet on whose books the popular TV show *The Flying Nun* was based. While growing up in Alexandria, Rocky had been an altar boy at St. Rita before going to West Point, where he graduated in 1959. He was as brilliant

Humbert Roque "Rocky" Versace, American hero, devout Catholic, and St. Rita parishioner. *U.S. Army.*

as he was determined. After graduation, he successfully completed Ranger training, and he mastered both the French and Vietnamese languages. And though he volunteered to serve in Vietnam, his greatest desire was to be a Maryknoll missionary priest: he had been accepted to its seminary following his service. In 1963, while serving with the 5th Special Forces Group (Green Berets), he was advising and organizing South Vietnamese militia units who were attacked by an overwhelming Viet Cong force. He provided covering fire to allow the militia troops to escape, but he was grievously wounded and captured.

For two years, he suffered torture and deprivation. Nonetheless, he could not be broken, and he was an inspiration to his fellow captive Americans. He attempted escape numerous times. Finally, in 1965, his captors executed him. His body was never recovered, although there is an empty grave at Arlington National Cemetery with a cross that bears his name. In 2002, he was posthumously awarded the Congressional Medal of Honor. Each year, on Memorial Day, St. Rita Parish youth groups honor his memory at his statue at the nearby Mount Vernon Recreation Center.

The heroism of Rocky Versace while a prisoner of war in Vietnam revealed a profound faith. Over the course of the 1960s and subsequent times, the St. Rita faithful would walk a path that would at times be challenging. But they could find examples to follow in stalwart souls such as Monsignor Gallagher, the good Sisters of St. Joseph, and Rocky Versace. These men and women were shining examples of faith to guide the parish in the tumultuous years to follow.

A TIME OF CHANGE, 1967–1986

Monsignor Gallagher's Final Year

St. Augustine famously said, "Bad times, hard times, this is what people keep saying; but let us live well, and times shall be good. We are the times: Such as we are, such are the times." In many respects, the community of St. Rita's in the late 1960s was very much of its time. The events of that crowded decade were mirrored in the ordinary life of the parish, and in particular, the year 1967 saw many significant milestones symbolizing that optimistic period of transition.

Although he had petitioned for retirement in early 1967, Monsignor Gallagher was to remain at St. Rita Parish for several more months as pastor emeritus in residence. During his final year at St. Rita's, he undertook two significant projects stemming from the reforms of the Second Vatican Council. The first was to establish a Parish Advisory Board on March 5. The board consisted of the leaders of the various parish ministries and apostolates. The board included representatives from the Sisters of St. Joseph, Women's Club, the Holy Name Society, the Catholic Youth Organization (CYO), the Christian Family Movement, the Confraternity of Christian Doctrine (CCD), the Home and School Association, the Boy Scouts, and the Girl Scouts.

The Parish Advisory Board formally recognized the contributions of the lay faithful that had developed and grown organically over the preceding decades. The Women's Sodality had borne much of the responsibility for

Parish Advisory Board in 1974. *St. Rita Parish Archives*.

Women's Conference in 1970s. *St. Rita Parish Archives*.

maintenance and upkeep of the facilities. The Holy Name Society often provided skilled labor for construction projects and repairs. The Christian Family Movement organized collections for charity. The CCD, CYO, and Scouts were naturally concerned with youth ministry. All these activities would continue in this new era focused on the role of the laity in the Church, albeit under a more centralized organizational structure overseen by the pastor.

The second major project of Monsignor Gallagher's final year was a renovation of the sanctuary to allow for Masses to be said with the priest facing the people, in the spirit of liturgical changes that followed the Second Vatican Council. Monsignor Gallagher commissioned the reconstruction of the altar with great sensitivity to the original architecture. This work was accompanied by the introduction of commentary during Mass explaining the liturgy. A folk band provided the musical accompaniment for the first time in September 1967 at the 9:30 a.m. Mass.

In his final years, Monsignor Gallagher's vision began to fail, but he still had a sense of humor regarding the infirmities of age, quipping to a parishioner that his familiar green car and his eyesight "gave out at the same time." After serving the St. Rita's community for two decades, he departed for what would prove to be a brief retirement. Shortly after returning to his native Pennsylvania, he passed away on February 9, 1968. His funeral was attended by three bishops and clergy from all along the Eastern Seaboard, and his mortal remains were interred at what is now Fairfax Memorial Park, which has become the final resting place of many other notable Catholic public figures from the region. To honor his memory, parishioners raised $8,000 for the purchase of a new organ, and memorial plaques honoring both Monsignor Koster and him—the parish's founder and builder—are found on the church's narthex (vestibule) wall.

GLOBAL CHANGE

In October 1967, St. Rita Parish received its first transitional deacon, Reverend George Zahn, who was ordained a priest for the Diocese of Richmond the following year. The year 1968 was one of upheavals and turmoil around the world, with the Vietnam War at its height, student strikes, revolutionary fervor, Communist repression in Czechoslovakia, the assassinations of Martin Luther King Jr. and Robert F. Kennedy, numerous

Traffic stopped on Shirley Highway at Washington and Old Dominion Railroad in 1960s. *VirginiaPlaces.org.*

riots in the United States and abroad, and the dissent following the publication of Pope St. Paul VI's encyclical *Humanae Vitae*, which reaffirmed the Church's long-held position against artificial contraception. Some of the shock waves of the era were felt at St. Rita. The notes of the Parish Advisory Board mention a clothing drive for people who lost their homes in the Washington, D.C. riots. And as a matter of more pedestrian concern, the Washington and Old Dominion Railroad ceased operations after years of declining traffic, leaving the St. Rita community without rail service until the long-delayed opening of the Potomac Yard Metro station in 2023.

As examples of the change within the Church following the Second Vatican Council, the year 1968 also saw changes in parish worship. A lay-run liturgy committee was formed and incorporated as part of the Parish Advisory Board. In an apparent effort at ecumenism, and not without protestation, solemn processions on Marian feasts ceased. First Communion became a more individualized rite of passage, with each child preparing with his or her family and then receiving the Eucharist when the family felt the child was ready, although this practice would be discontinued by 1974.

In the following year, a Legion of Mary chapter and a fifty-plus club were founded. Sister Cecilia of the Sisters of St. Joseph was appointed as the youth choir director. The Parish Advisory Board was also reorganized under a new constitution and was led by an elected layperson, freeing the priests to direct their energies toward the spiritual needs of the parish. To that end, the new constitution was formally adopted on March 30, 1969, and William Grant was elected chairman.

New Forms of Lay Participation

In 1970, Pope Paul VI promulgated a new Roman missal. Whereas the period immediately following the Second Vatican Council was marked by innovations and experimentation, the new missal sought to "express more clearly the holy things they signify, to encourage devout and active participation of the faithful, and to open the treasures of the Bible more lavishly." In practice at St. Rita, cantors no longer wore a clerical cassock and surplice, and a communal penance service was held for the first time. Some parishioners embraced the changes as fresh and overdue in the liturgy; others questioned them as unnecessary and unworthy of serious worship. As an example of the evangelical and ecumenical spirit of the postconciliar era, a Mass was offered at the now-demolished Landmark Mall during Lent as part of a "Marketplace Ministries" series in conjunction with other denominations.

The Parish Advisory Board was deeply involved in every aspect of the administration of the parish during this time. In Richmond, the Office of Lay Activities monitored each parish to ensure that the laity were being consulted in planning and decision-making. One notable example was the installation of an air conditioning system. Planning had begun in 1969,

St. Rita religion teachers in workshop. *St. Rita Parish Archives.*

Left: Father Thomas Casey. *St. Rita Parish Archives.*

Right: Sister Ann Bernard. *St. Rita Parish Archives.*

and the work was completed in the winter of 1970 after raising funds through a special collection drive.

The early 1970s also saw greater involvement of the laity in religious education. The St. Rita Parish Advisory Board included a religious education committee to help develop new programs and pedagogies. In 1970, Sister Therese Immaculate, SSJ, became the first full-time director of religious education. She was succeeded by Sister Marie Josephine, SSJ, in 1972. That same year, the Parish Advisory Board also advocated for improved education about human sexuality at the parish school, and priests in Northern Virginia adopted a statement explaining Catholic teaching on abortion and contraception to be distributed to engaged couples in response to a Virginia law mandating that court clerks provide information about contraceptives along with marriage licenses. The board petitioned for the priests' statement to be made a diocesan policy early in 1973, just weeks before the Supreme Court issued its decision in *Roe v. Wade.*

There were several associate pastors during the late 1960s and early 1970s. Father Edmund Marroni was succeeded by Father James Fallon in 1968. Father Fallon was followed by Father Don Hanna from 1968 to 1969 and Father Thomas Casey, who was appointed in 1969. Father Eugene Poirier, SJ, was also in residence from 1970 to 1972, and the Capuchin fathers continued to assist with Masses and CCD classes, particularly Father Peter Damian, OFM, Cap., who was assigned to St. Rita's from 1969 to 1973. Father Stewart Culkin was also in residence at St. Rita's as a seminarian in 1969–70 prior to his diaconal ordination. In 1968, Sister Catherine Rosarii Cawley was appointed as principal. She was succeeded in 1972 by Sister Ann Bernard Carlin, who served until 1978.

Rising and Falling Tides

Father (later Monsignor) Francis Bradican. *St. Rita Parish Archives.*

In 1972, Father Francis Bradican arrived at St. Rita from St. Bernadette Parish, which he had built from the ground up as its founding pastor. He was born in Dunmore, Pennsylvania, and attended St. Charles Seminary in Catonsville, as well as the University of Louvain in Belgium and the North American College in Rome. There he was ordained to the priesthood in 1936, three months earlier than the rest of his class, because he was in poor health and not expected to survive. Despite this brush with death, he would have a long and eventful life, to include nearly fifteen years of service at St. Rita.

Father Bradican's first projects after arriving at St. Rita were to attend to much-needed maintenance of the church and school. In the church, he had the plaster painted and the stonework cleaned. In the school, the Building Committee organized volunteers to renovate the school hall under the leadership of their chairman, Douglas Foran. By the time of St. Rita's golden jubilee in 1974, the facilities had been thoroughly updated.

The 1970s were a difficult period for the community surrounding St. Rita. The wartime and postwar population boom that had seen the parish grow from the 1940s through the 1960s was now ebbing. A quite literal tide was rising in its place: the extensive deforestation and paving of the area that had begun in the 1930s was now contributing to increased runoff and more severe flooding of Four Mile Run. Particularly devastating were Hurricane Agnes in 1972 and Hurricane Eloise in 1975.

Above: Saint Rita School's graduating class of 1974. *St. Rita Parish Archives.*

Opposite: Flooding from Hurricane Eloise in 1975. *Historic Alexandria.*

Thanks to the foresight of its builders, the church remained unharmed by the recurring floodwaters, but the flooding dampened the economic vitality of the neighborhood. A contemporary article in the *Catholic Virginian* about a social services center on Mount Vernon Avenue operated by the Diocese of Richmond described the area as a "ghetto," much to the consternation of the local citizenry. The Vernon Theater, a center of community activity, closed its doors in 1976. A *Washington Post* article from 1979 included interviews with struggling businesses in the Arlandria shopping center. Most merchants had a bleak outlook, operating on a week-to-week basis, although one managed to stay open: Robcyns, the school uniform supplier, which eventually relocated to the Bradlee shopping center elsewhere in Alexandria before it finally closed in 2024.

With the decline in the community, the parish rolls began to shrink: from 890 families in 1960 to 785 in the jubilee year of 1974. The enrollment of

Opposite, top: Eagle Scout banquet in Parish Center. *St. Rita Parish Archives*.

Opposite, middle: St. Rita's CYO boys' basketball team, circa 1978. *St. Rita Parish Archives.*

Opposite, bottom: Production of *Godspell* by St. Rita folk band. *St. Rita Parish Archives*.

Left: Banner for Golden Jubilee in 1974. *St. Rita Parish Archives.*

the school had also declined to 395 students. Children from Bolling Air Force Base were bused in, which helped keep enrollment up, but in 1970, two-thirds of students from the base declined to re-enroll. Although it had been Monsignor Gallagher's dream to provide free education, Father Bradican had no option but to increase tuition despite the hardship it placed on many families already struggling with the economic malaise of that decade. Meanwhile, the deprivations of the less fortunate in the community were mounting. Parish Advisory Board minutes from that time include frequent appeals for food and clothing to assist a growing number of families in need.

Under the leadership of Father Bradican, the faithful of St. Rita were undeterred by this gloomy picture. The Women's Club organized craft bazaars, card parties, and an art show. In 1974, James Trabert was

Opposite, top: Procession for Golden Jubilee. *St. Rita Parish Archives*.

Opposite, bottom: Celebration of the Golden Jubilee Mass. *St. Rita Parish Archives.*

Above: Procession for Golden Jubilee. *St. Rita Parish Archives*.

appointed as the new music director and organized new men's and women's choirs that sang Latin plainchant as well as contemporary hymns. The folk music band also organized a production of *Godspell*. A major milestone was achieved when all debts from the construction of the church and school were paid in full. There was much to celebrate at the jubilee Masses on May 19 commemorating the building of the original church in 1914 and September 21 celebrating the founding of the parish in 1924. For the May anniversary, there was also a traditional blessing of roses, a devotion long associated with St. Rita.

Vocation Stories

Through an era of change, St. Rita continued to produce vocations. The Rippy family settled in Alexandria in 1965, and Robert Rippy became a parishioner and student. He remembers serving Mass for Father Bradican, who became a good family friend. He remembers the high quality of the education provided and that, even amid the late '60s upheavals, the Sisters kept tight discipline—the boys could not loosen up their ties at any time during the school day.

Ultimately, Rippy went to seminary at St. Charles Borromeo in Philadelphia, one of the three seminaries where the diocese would send men to study for the priesthood (the others being Mount St. Mary's in Emmitsburg, Maryland, and the North American College in Rome). He was ordained in 1984 and offered his first Mass at St. Rita. Father Rippy's mother was a devout "classic Italian mother." His father, a retired marine, however, was not Catholic. However, in the 1980s, his father "covertly" began instruction in the faith. A few years later, Father Rippy baptized his father—as he jokingly recalls, the "biggest baby he ever baptized," and gave him First Holy Communion.

Another vocation story of the period was that of Father Andrew Fisher. Born in 1972, he grew up on nearby Old Dominion Boulevard, attended St. Rita from kindergarten, and was an altar boy. He was also a serious professional baseball pitching prospect and attended Mount St. Mary University as a star player (having little to no idea of the seminary there). Holy seminarians and friends there helped prompt his calling to the priesthood, and he also would offer his first Mass at St. Rita. Later, as pastor of St. Ambrose Parish in Annandale, he would oversee the building of its beautiful new church. Reportedly, he could be seen from time to time coming back to St. Rita for inspiration and ideas, and visitors to both churches can perhaps see some subtle similarities between the two!

A New Diocese and New Immigrants

During the golden jubilee year of 1974, the parishioners of St. Rita were given further reason to celebrate with the establishment of the Diocese of Arlington on August 13 and the selection of St. Thomas More Church as the cathedral of the new see. Given the diocese's proximity to the capital, it was altogether fitting that St. Thomas More, the patron saint of lawyers and statesmen, would be the patron saint of the diocese.

As bishop of Arlington from 1974 until 1983, Bishop Thomas Welsh created six new parishes. He also established the Office of Migration and Refugee Services in 1975 to assist refugees fleeing Vietnam after the fall of Saigon. Many came to settle in Clarendon's "Little Saigon" and in the

Arlandria neighborhood around St. Rita. Providing resettlement assistance was one of the many social outreach ministries in the parish at that time. One parishioner recalled at a food drive at St. Rita in 2023 that she was forever indebted to Catholic Charities for saving her life as a little girl when her father was executed by the Communists.

In 1979, the Salvadoran Civil War began with a military-backed coup leading to guerrilla warfare, brutal repressions, and retaliations with huge numbers of civilian casualties. In 1980, the assassination of St. Óscar Romero and other Catholic clerics and religious sisters engaged in relief efforts shocked the world. Civil war in El Salvador, along with "disappearances" and overall economic decline in that beleaguered nation, would continue through the 1980s, leading to increasing numbers of refugees seeking asylum in the United States. With the completion of levees along Four Mile Run in the same year, previously flood-prone sections of Arlandria were now more attractive for these newest arrivals, who gave their adopted home the nickname "Chirilagua," which has since been recognized by the City of Alexandria as part of the official place name.

Throughout the decade, St. Rita Parish saw many new arrivals but also the passing away of parishioners who had first petitioned for the original mission. Local newspapers of this time contained obituaries for first-generation immigrants from Ireland, Italy, and Germany who attended St. Rita for decades. In most cases, their children and grandchildren resettled elsewhere, while new immigrants from Vietnam and El Salvador added to the melting pot of different cultures that have called the parish home. Indeed, the melting pot was a very literal one when the Home and School Association held an international potluck dinner in 1979.

The Last Monsignor

In 1976, Father Casey was reassigned as pastor of St. Charles Borromeo Parish, leaving Father Bradican alone as pastor responsible for the needs of more than 750 families and a school with 400 students. With the needs of the community greater than ever, parishioners at St. Rita petitioned Bishop Welsh for a new assistant pastor to be assigned to the parish, and in 1978, Father Franklyn McAfee was assigned as priest-in-residence. In addition to his duties in the chancery at the Office for Family Life, which he founded in 1977, he also led RCIA classes at St. Rita. After leaving St.

Monday   November 24, 1980

CELEBRANT   Bishop Thomas J. Welsh
                         Bishop of Arlington

PASTOR   Rev. Francis L. Bradican
                         St. Rita's Parish

PRINCIPAL   Sister Marie St. Paul S.S.J.
                         St. Rita's School

COORDINATOR   Mrs. Kathleen Durso

INSTRUCTORS   Sister Mary Gillespie S.S.J.

                         Mrs. Gina Sarrasin

MUSIC   Mr. C. William Rohrer, Director
                         St. Rita's Choir

                         Mrs. Catherine DeMetz
                         St. Rita's School Music Teacher

                         Dorothy Braun
                         Organist

RECEPTION   Mrs Carol Gray

                         Sixth Grade Parents, Teachers, and Students

TO EACH PERSON THE MANIFESTATION OF THE SPIRIT IS GIVEN FOR THE COMMON GOOD.

Flyer for Confirmation in 1980. *St. Rita Parish Archives.*

Rita in 1983, Father McAfee served as pastor of several parishes before retiring in 2009.

In 1986, Father Bradican received the title of monsignor shortly before retiring as pastor of St. Rita Parish. During his retirement, he lived as priest-in-residence at Holy Spirit Parish in Annandale. By the time of his death on March 31, 2003, at the age of ninety-two, he had earned the distinction of being one of the longest-serving priests in the diocese with a career spanning sixty-five years.

By the end of the 1970s and into the early to mid-1980s, St. Rita Parish was a very different place than it had been in the 1960s. Mirroring national trends, crime in the neighboring community had risen dramatically. The Parish Advisory Board minutes from 1979 recorded a concern familiar with parishioners today—of speeding cars cutting through the alleyways adjacent to the church. In the middle of the 1980s, the use of crack cocaine became prevalent despite frequent police arrests. Drug dealers often simply relocated from one house to another, often on the same block, making little effort to conceal their activities from law-abiding neighbors. However, through each new wave of settlement and resettlement, and despite the decline in public safety, St. Rita Church remained a steady rock and refuge in a world beset by storms and tribulations.

ST. RITA

---◆---

LA COMUNIDAD DE HISPANOHABLANTES

UNA NUEVA COMUNIDAD

Durante la década de los 1980, los inmigrantes de El Salvador fueron unos de los primeros grupos de Hispanohablantes que se arraigaron en los vecindarios alrededor de Santa Rita. Muy pronto empezaron a radicarse nuevos grupos también de Nicaragua, Guatemala, Panamá y otros lugares. Muchos llegaron huyendo de la opresión política, dejando atrás todas sus posesiones, sus profesiones, y a veces también a sus familias. Otros buscaron mejores posibilidades económicas, ya que los conflictos y la violencia recortaron las oportunidades en sus países de origen.

En 1984, el obispo asignó al Padre John O'Hara y el Reverendo Guillermo Casas a la Parroquia de Santa Rita para administrar a esta nueva y creciente comunidad. Más tarde el Padre O'Hara llegó a ser el Director de Caridades Católicas y fue misionero en Bánica en la República Dominicana. En 1986 cuando el Padre Martin McGuill fue nombrado párroco, la Misa se ofrecía en español cada Domingo con unos cientos de personas en la asamblea. Después, se formó un coro hispano.

En 1988, el Padre Francisco Méndez de Dios, originalmente de España, fue nombrado párroco asociado. Él nació en 1935 en Galicia y fue ordenado sacerdote en Madrid en 1960. Llegó a los Estados Unidos en 1979 y fue incardinado en la Diócesis de Arlington en 1986. Permaneció en Santa Rita hasta 1995, y la última parte de su tiempo estuvo como sacerdote en residencia mientras servía en el tribunal diocesano. Luego sirvió como vicario parroquial en las parroquias de San Carlos Borromeo en Arlington y Todos los Santos en Manassas, y ahora vive en la Villa de Retiro de Santa Rosa de Lima. También la parroquia recibió a José Pardo como diácono permanente y el Diácono Pardo fue muy activo en el ministerio a la comunidad hispana, un papel que continuó después de mudarse a la Parroquia de la Natividad en Burke. Se retiró en 2015 y ahora reside en Falls Church.

En 1989, mientras Santa Rita celebraba el 75 aniversario desde la fundación de la misión parroquial, el Padre McGuill organizó una fiesta en el césped frente a la rectoría con música, comida y juegos que representante la variedad de culturas de la parroquia. Los cambios en la ley de inmigración en 1990 llevaron a un crecimiento aún mayor de la comunidad, especialmente en los feligreses de El Salvador, ya que a los refugiados se les otorgó el estatus de protección temporal. Para aquellos que llegaban a los Estados Unidos sin casi nada, la Hermana Brigid dirigió una iniciativa para ayudar a los recién llegados a encontrar casas y amueblarlas.

A finales de la década de 1990, los negocios que atendían a la comunidad de hispanohablantes comenzaron a aparecer, lo cual reanimó la sección de Mount Vernon Avenue que se había deteriorado por las inundaciones frecuentes en la década de 1970. En Santa Rita, surgieron los apostolados laicos tal como la Legión de María y el grupo de jóvenes adultos que también acogieron a los jóvenes de los recién llegados. Durante muchos años había un festival hispano anual y un bazar en el otoño donde los vendedores exhibían artes y artesanías tradicionales. Al igual que con todos los grupos de inmigrantes, la comunidad de hispanohablantes plantó raíces profundas en su hogar adoptivo.

In el año 2000, el Padre Dennis Donahue fue nombrado párroco y con él empezó una tradición de asignar un cura bilingüe en Santa Rita la cual ha perdurado con el Padre Daniel Gee (párroco de 2010 a 2021) y Padre Christopher Christensen (párroco de 2021 hasta el presente), que son bilingües los dos.

VIEJAS TRADICIONES EN UNA NUEVA TIERRA

A través de los años, se va añadiendo nuevos costumbres y tradiciones a la vida parroquial, enriqueciendo enormemente la vida spiritual de los feligreses y algunos se recuerdan en los capítulos siguientes de este historial. Para las nuevas generaciones de descendientes nacidos en los Estados Unidos, muchos de los cuales se han mudado a otros vecindarios lejanos, estas tradiciones proporcionan un vínculo importante con la cultura y la historia de sus antepasados y con la parroquia de Santa Rita. Una de las fiestas más importantes de El Salvador es la fiesta de Nuestra Señora Reina de la Paz que se celebra el 21 de noviembre. En 1682, se descubrió una misteriosa caja en una playa. Al principio no se podía abrir y la transportaron en burro. En medio del camino, el animal se detuvo y no se movía. Esta vez pudieron abrir la caja y encontraron que contenía una imagen de Nuestra Señora con el Niño Jesús. Al escuchar del descubrimiento, los habitantes de la región que estaban en medio de una sangrienta guerra depusieron sus armas, y así la imagen fue nombrada Nuestra Señora de la Paz. El aniversario del descubrimiento se conmemora con una celebración que dura un mes y que culmina en un carnaval con desfiles, música, baile y fuegos artificiales.

Hay otro milagro que está entrelazado con esta Santa Virgen que se celebra en Santa Rita. Al lugar donde se detuvo el burro fue construida la Catedral de San Miguel. En

St. Rita Parish Spanish-speaking community youth with Bishop Joseph J. Madera, Auxiliary Bishop of the Archdiocese for the Military Services, USA, circa early to mid-1990s. *St. Rita Parish Archives.*

Re-creating the miracle of Guadalupe. *Mary Pat Schlickenmaier.*

1787, los ciudadanos de ese pueblo buscaron refugio después en la Catedral cuando el volcán de Chaparrastique entró en erupción. Se dice que cuando la gente rezó por la intercesión de Nuestra Señora de la Paz, la lava cambiaba de dirección y así se salvó el pueblo. Este milagro llevó al reconocimiento oficial de la imagen por parte del Papa Benedicto XV en 1921. El volcán sigue activo y ha entrado en erupción en 2002, 2013 y, más recientemente, en 2022. En la parroquia de Santa Rita, la fiesta se celebra con una procesión que ha incluido una recreación del volcán.

Una de las tradiciones recién de la comunidad Hispana de Santa Rita es la Via Crucis en Vivo, que comenzó en 2006 y que recuerda las representaciones de la Pasión de Cristo que abundan en las calles del mundo hispanohablante desde hace siglos. El P. Daniel Gee también inició una Misa especial para la fiesta de Nuestra Señora de Guadalupe con un grupo de mariachi haciendo acompañamiento musical.

La comunidad de hispanohablantes ha enriquecido enormemente la vida parroquial y, a su vez, Santa Rita ha proporcionado un hogar espiritual a tantos en nuestra comunidad. Esta realidad se ve en la réplica de la tilma famosa de San Juan Diego, impresa con la imagen de la Santísima Virgen en Guadalupe, que está en el nártex de la iglesia, y también en la estatua de Nuestra Señora de Guadalupe que se encuentra al lado de la parroquia. Ambos nos recuerdan todos, y de manera especial la comunidad hispana de Santa Rita, muchos de los cuales han viajado de tan lejos y han sufrido tanto, lo que la Santísima Virgen le dijo a San Juan Diego hace tanto tiempo en 1531. Le dijo que no dejara que nada lo perturbara, porque "¿No estoy yo aquí, que soy tu Madre?"

THE SPANISH-SPEAKING COMMUNITY

A NEW COMMUNITY

During the 1980s, immigrants from El Salvador were some of the first Spanish speakers to settle in the area around St. Rita. They were soon joined by others from Nicaragua, Guatemala, Panama, and elsewhere. Many were forced to flee oppression, leaving their jobs and all their possessions behind—and sometimes family members as well. Others sought better economic prospects as war and violence led to diminished opportunities in their native lands.

Fathers John O'Hara and Guillermo Casas were assigned to St. Rita Parish in 1984 to minister to this new and growing community. Father O'Hara would later go on to serve as the director of Catholic Charities and then as a missionary in Bánica in the Dominican Republic. By 1986, when

Father Martin McGuill was appointed as pastor, Mass was being offered in Spanish every Sunday, with several hundred people in the congregation. Soon there was also a choir for that Mass.

In 1988, Father Francisco Mendez de Dios, originally from Spain, was appointed as associate pastor. He was born in 1935 in Galicia and was ordained in Madrid in 1960. He moved to the United States in 1979 and was incardinated in the Diocese of Arlington in 1986. He remained at St. Rita until 1995, with the latter part of that time being priest-in-residence while serving the tribunal. He went on to serve as parochial vicar at St. Charles Borromeo and All Saints Parishes and now lives at the St. Rose of Lima Retirement Villa. Also, Deacon Jose Pardo came and was very active in ministering to the Spanish-speaking community, a role he continued after moving to Nativity Parish in Burke. He retired in 2015 and now resides in Falls Church.

In 1989, as St. Rita celebrated the seventy-fifth anniversary of the mission church, Father McGuill hosted a fiesta on the lawn in front of the rectory with music, food, and games representing the many cultures within the parish. Changes to immigration law in 1990 led to even more growth in the Spanish-speaking community, especially from El Salvador as refugees were granted temporary protected status. For those coming to the United States with almost nothing, one of the Sisters of St. Joseph at St. Rita, Sister Brigid, led outreach efforts to help find homes and set up furnishings for new arrivals.

By the end of the 1990s, businesses catering to the Spanish-speaking community had started opening, revitalizing the section of Mount Vernon Avenue that had been so devastated by frequent flooding in the 1970s. At St. Rita, ministries such as the Legion of Mary and the young adults group welcomed the younger generation of new arrivals. For many years, there was an annual Hispanic festival and a bazaar in the fall where vendors showcased traditional arts and crafts. As with every group of immigrants, the Spanish-speaking community put down deep roots in their adopted home.

In 2000, Father Dennis Donahue was appointed pastor, and he began the tradition of a bilingual pastor serving at St. Rita that has since endured. Both Father Daniel Gee (pastor, 2010–21) and Father Christopher Christensen (pastor, 2021–present) are bilingual as well. These pastors have furthered the outreach to the Spanish-speaking community, and their efforts are detailed in later chapters of the history.

OLD TRADITIONS IN A NEW LAND

Throughout the years, new customs and traditions have been added at the parish, greatly enriching the spiritual life of all the faithful, some of which are recalled in later chapters of this history. For the new generations of descendants born in the United States, many of whom have moved to far-off neighborhoods, these traditions provide an important link to the culture and history of their forefathers and to St. Rita Parish. One of the most important festivals in El Salvador is celebrated on November 21 in honor of Our Lady Queen of Peace, and it is also celebrated at St Rita. In 1682, a mysterious box was discovered on a beach. At first it could not be opened, so it was transported on a donkey. Along the way, the donkey stopped and would not move, and the box was then opened to find it contained an image of Our Lady with the Christ Child. Upon hearing of the discovery, the inhabitants of the region who had been fighting a bloody war laid down their weapons, and thus the image was named Our Lady of Peace. The anniversary of the discovery is marked with a month-long celebration that culminates in a carnival with parades, music, dancing, and fireworks.

There is another miracle linked to this holy image that is celebrated at St. Rita. The place where the donkey stopped is now the Cathedral of San Miguel, and in 1787, the townspeople sought refuge there when the volcano of Chaparrastique erupted. It is said that when the people prayed for the intercession of Our Lady of Peace, the lava changed direction and spared the town. This miracle led to Pope Benedict XV's official recognition of the image in 1927. The volcano is still active and has erupted in 2002, 2013, and, most recently, in 2022. At St. Rita Parish, the feast is celebrated with a procession, sometimes including a re-creation of the volcano.

Among the recent traditions of St. Rita's Hispanic community is the live Stations of the Cross, which began in 2006 and recall the Passion plays that have abounded in the streets of the Spanish-speaking world for centuries. Father Gee also started a special, early morning Mass on the feast of Our Lady of Guadalupe, with a mariachi band providing the musical accompaniment.

The Spanish-speaking community has greatly enriched parish life, and in turn, St. Rita has provided a spiritual home to so many in our community. This reality is seen in the replica of the famous *tilma* left by the Blessed Mother at Guadalupe, placed in the church narthex and in the statue of Our Lady of Guadalupe, which stands in the rectory yard. Both remind all of us, and in a special way the Spanish-speaking St. Rita community, many of whom have traveled so far and endured so much, of the Blessed Virgin's words of comfort to Saint Juan Diego in 1531. She told him not to let anything disturb him, for "Am I not here, I who am your mother?"

FURTHER GROWTH, 1986–2000

EFFORTS AT FURTHER GROWTH

On March 18, 1986, one day before the Solemnity of Saint Joseph, a five-member Diocese of Arlington Clergy Personnel Board comprising Monsignor John Hannon, Reverend Alan Lee, Reverend Joseph Loftus, Reverend Robert Cilinski, and Reverend Stewart Culkin met with eighty-five St. Rita parishioners to evaluate and make recommendations about clergy staffing for the parish's future. Bishop John R. Keating had just named Father Francis L. Bradican as monsignor five weeks earlier on his seventy-fifth birthday.

By this time, St. Rita Parish consisted of 624 registered families of diverse backgrounds that included, according to the Clergy Personnel Board, "many older people, Hispanics, a range of socio-economic backgrounds, and young married couples who [were] beginning to move back into the area." On average, one nuptial Mass and one funeral Mass were celebrated at St. Rita Church each month.

The Spanish-speaking community continued to grow. As many as three hundred people attended the Spanish-language Mass each Sunday. Religious education classes were held three times a week for the Spanish-speaking community. In August 1988, the parish established a Court of the Catholic Daughters—a "charitable, benevolent, and patriotic sorority for Catholic ladies" dedicated to the principles of "unity and charity"—for Spanish-

Left: St. Rita students visit the U.S. Capitol with Virginia's 8th Congressional District Representative James P. Moran, 1991. *St. Rita Parish Archives.*

Below: Sister Frances Amata Curran with St. Rita students. *Mary Pat Schlickenmaier.*

speaking women from Catholic parishes throughout Alexandria who were at least eighteen years old.

St. Rita School remained a focal point for the parish during this time, regardless of the decline in student enrollment. At the school's core were seven Sisters of St. Joseph and ten other lay teachers entrusted with educating the minds and souls of 251 students and 41 Confraternity of Christian Doctrine (CCD) students. Many of these students were part of U.S. Air Force families who resided at Bolling Air Force Base on the east bank of the Potomac River in southeast Washington, D.C., and who availed themselves of round-trip bus transportation between Bolling and St. Rita School.

Most of the Clergy Personnel Board meeting attendees were long-standing parishioners who were over fifty years old. Many of them complimented Monsignor Bradican for his accomplishments as pastor, especially for making necessary adjustments to the parish's organization to meet the community's evolving needs. In a discernably positive tone, they conveyed a range of views on the future direction of the parish. Many of them indicated the need to preserve traditional devotional and liturgical practices, which, among other things, they believed well suited the church's Gothic architecture. They also recognized the need to attract the next generation of single young adults and families to the parish. During the previous year (1985–86), one hundred new families registered with the parish, and the board noted the sentiment that "there is a need to get those people involved and stirred up." Some attendees expressed their satisfaction with the parish's "restful" environment, as well as their preference against any "fireworks" going forward.

During the meeting, a few vocal St. Rita parishioners from the Spanish-speaking community expressed their gratitude to the parish for its outreach and emphasized its importance to their community. Aggressive evangelization by local non-Catholic churches, particularly Grace Episcopal Church, located across West Glebe Road from St. Rita Parish, underscored the need for the parish to continue to engage the local Spanish-speaking community.

Regarding St. Rita School, the attendees hoped for a pastor who would be dedicated to Catholic education and who would improve and expand the school for the future. It was suggested that the parish convert the school's annex to a gymnasium. In a perhaps more pressing matter, the Sisters of St. Joseph planned to continue to staff the school for the time being, but they indicated that they might need to withdraw their service in the future.

The 1986 board thereby set a baseline for St. Rita Parish's continued growth. The board's work also led to the appointment of a new pastor for St. Rita Parish, Father Martin F. McGuill, who served from 1986 to 1992. An air force chaplain, he served as a military chaplain at Arlington National Cemetery for many years. He also held a doctorate in canon law from the Pontifical University of St. Thomas in Rome and, prior to coming to the parish, served on the diocesan tribunal. He thus came with rich, varied, practical experience, ready to minister to St. Rita families.

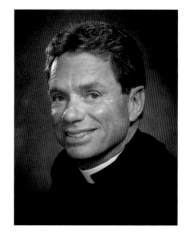

Father Martin F. McGuill, pastor, 1986–92. *St. Luke Parish, McLean, Virginia.*

CELEBRATING A DIAMOND JUBILEE

In May 1988, St. Rita commenced a yearlong celebration in advance of a seventy-fifth anniversary, its Diamond Jubilee of sorts—not of its establishment as a parish per se, but as the date when Masses began to be offered in the first church. And in just two years, registered membership had continued to grow by some 16 percent to about 750 families, mostly from the north Alexandria and south Arlington area.

The plans for the St. Rita Diamond Jubilee celebrations included two major fundraising goals: to establish an endowment for the maintenance of the classic Gothic church and the parish buildings and to complete an earlier-launched fundraising campaign for a new pipe organ in time for the jubilee in June 1989. The year of planned events included two art and antique shows and sales, concerts, a car raffle, a lecture series, a parish and community fiesta, and a western-style hoedown.

There were multiple events for the Diamond Jubilee during the first weekend of June 1989. The official celebration began with a Vigil Mass on Saturday evening, followed by a parish fiesta on Sunday afternoon. The fiesta included a raffle for a 1989 Chevrolet Beretta, donated by the John Koons Junior Chevrolet dealership and presented by Billy Kilmer, former quarterback for the Washington Redskins and a local football hero. The

DIAMOND JUBILEE MASS

JUNE 3, 1989

St. Rita's Church
Alexandria, Virginia

Left: Program for St. Rita Parish's Diamond Jubilee Mass on June 3, 1989. *St. Rita Parish Archives.*

Below: The *Arlington Catholic Herald* highlights Advent at St. Rita Parish, 1990. *From the* Arlington Catholic Herald.

ARLINGTON CATHOLIC HERALD

A Blessed Christmas To All

Christmas Comes To St. Rita Church

St. Rita Church in Alexandria prepares for the Christmas season and the birth of Christ with a brightly decorated tree (above) and the traditional creche scene (below). The church is located at Russell and South Glebe Roads. Father Martin McGuill is pastor.

festivities also included "A Taste of Arlandria," provided by local restaurants; rides; live music; dancing; and "lots, lots, more!"

On Saturday, June 3, 1989, hundreds of longtime St. Rita parishioners, including ninety-one-year-old Camille DeLane, the first St. Rita organist, and a number of newcomers filled the church's sanctuary for the Diamond Jubilee Mass. Bishop John Keating, Father McGuill, and former St. Rita pastors concelebrated the Mass. Nationally renowned broadcast journalist Roger Mudd read the first reading, parishioner Aurora Rodriguez read the second reading in Spanish, and Deacon Jose I. Pardo read the Gospel. Former St. Rita associate pastor Father John T. O'Hara, who then served as the diocesan director of charities, delivered the homily, in which he reminded parishioners that they were continuing to build the church "through charity, justice, mercy, and peace."

After Mass, a four-member ensemble of mariachi musicians performed during a reception that set the tone for the next day's highly anticipated fiesta. The parish's weekly bulletin included a letter of congratulations to St. Rita Parish from President George H.W. Bush and First Lady Barbara Bush.

The following Sunday afternoon on the parish grounds and parking lot, the fiesta afforded hours of celebration for parishioners and community members alike. Parishioners served ethnic foods to the masses. Fiesta-goers bought highly popular straw hats. They marveled at the fast-paced footwork of dancers in native Latin American costumes. They admired children's faces painted by the careful hand of "Butterfly the Clown." Older children climbed aboard an Alexandria Fire Department truck, where they donned a firefighter's helmet and perhaps imagined dousing a smoky charcoal grill to gallantly save St. Rita Parish from ruin on its seventy-fifth anniversary.

A New Pipe Organ Is Installed

St. Rita Parish's long tradition of elevating worship through music began with a simple pump organ in the old church on Hickory Street. By the 1950s, in the new church, the parish had transitioned to a then-state-of-the art electric organ manufactured by the Allen Organ Company in Pennsylvania. This Allen electric organ, and another acquired in 1968 as a memorial to Monsignor Gallagher, suited St. Rita Parish's liturgies for many years until they quite literally began to fall out of tune.

At the time of the Clergy Personnel Board of St. Rita Parish in 1986, one-third of the parishioners surveyed about various parish programs evaluated the parish's liturgical music program as "good," whereas others believed that it needed improvement. And so, in 1987, a new season for liturgical music at St. Rita Parish began when Father McGuill hired Dr. Paul Skevington from his position as the assistant organist at the National Shrine of the Immaculate Conception in Washington to the part-time position of St. Rita Parish's director of music and organist. Dr. Skevington later gained full-time employment at St. Rita Parish by taking on the additional role of the parish's director of the Rite of Christian Initiation of Adults (RCIA) under the specialized guidance of Carmelite Father Ron Oakham, a member of the North American Forum on the Catechumenate, who also joined the parish choir.

Together, Father McGuill and Dr. Skevington masterfully orchestrated the replacement of the Allen electric organ with a pipe organ that suited St. Rita Parish's Gothic church. The parish's fundraising effort to purchase a new pipe organ in time for its Diamond Jubilee was a huge success. The generosity of St. Rita parishioners and others raised $185,000 toward the purchase of a magnificent pipe organ from Steiner-Reck Inc. of Louisville,

St. Rita Church music director Dr. Paul Skevington (*right*) and volunteers offload Steiner-Reck pipe organ components. *Paul Skevington.*

Kentucky, a premier organ-building company cofounded in 1968 by Pharis L. Steiner, who had previously established Steiner Organs Inc. in Ohio, and Gottfried Reck, an experienced organ builder of the Detlev Kleuker Organbrau in Germany.

Steiner-Reck's 29 Rank Tracker Organ, custom-built for St. Rita Church, took more than a year to emerge from concept to the choir loft. The instrument's components were designed, crafted, assembled, and perfected in Louisville, Kentucky, and then disassembled and delivered to St. Rita Church. More than twenty parishioners unloaded the organ's components from a truck parked on the south side of the church and carefully carried them inside, where they placed them in the nave and several rows of pews closest to the choir loft. A hydraulic lift was used to raise the organ's main components to the loft. For nearly two months, Steiner-Reck organ builders assembled the organ on-site at St. Rita Church.

The organ's installation included a specifications sheet on which Gottfried Reck wrote:

> When St. Rita's Parish presented us with the challenge to create a new musical instrument for its church, we set our goal: to follow precedents of old masters and apply them to today's needs. More specifically, we strove to build an organ which reflects the clarity of those played by Bach and his contemporaries, while also displaying the warmth of tone found in organs built later in the Romantic era.
>
> The result of this combination, we feel, can be appreciated as much in tonal palette and voicing, as in its physical construction and design.
>
> Using today's technology, complemented by those procedures of building organs which have not changed for centuries, results in a successful instrument with tonal and technical resources that let various compositional styles be adequately accommodated.
>
> The visual design reflects this approach. It harmoniously combines contemporary elements and traditional motifs.
>
> The low profile, detached console, with its eight-level memory system and touch plate controls, affords the player/director convenience and balance.
>
> The success of this project was due, not only to the variety of materials and development in technology, but more so to the talents, ideas, and dedication of the many people at St. Rita's Parish and Steiner-Reck, Inc.
>
> St. Rita's Church has an organ of which to be proud. We hope it will be a source of inspiration to all…listeners, organists, and composers.

SPECIFICATIONS

Steiner-Reck 29 Rank Tracker Organ

GREAT

16'	Gedacktpommer
8'	Principal
8'	Rohrfloete
4'	Octave
4'	Hohlfloete
2'	Superoctave
2 ⅔'	Sesqualtera II
1 ⅓'	Mixture IV–V
8'	Trumpet

SWELL

8'	Koppelfloete
8'	Celeste T.C.
4'	Principal
4'	Spitzfloete
2'	Italian Principal
1 ⅓'	Quinte
1'	Mixture IV–V
8'	Hautbois
4'	Schalmei

Tremulant

PEDAL

16'	Bourdon
8'	Principal
8'	Bourdon
4'	Choralbass II
16'	Posaune

ACCESSORIES

Swell to Great
Great to Pedal
Swell to Pedal
Zimbelstern

*W*hen St. Rita's Parish presented us with the challenge to create a new musical instrument for its church, we first set our goal: to follow precedents of the old masters and apply them to today's needs. More specifically, we strove to build an organ which reflects the clarity of those played by Bach and his contemporaries, while also displaying the warmth of tone found in organs built later in the Romantic era.

The result of this combination, we feel, can be appreciated as much in its tonal palette and voicing, as in its physical construction and visual design.

Using today's technology, complimented by those procedures of building organs which have not changed for centuries, results in a successful instrument with tonal and technical resources that let various compositional styles be adequately accommodated.

The visual design reflects this approach. It harmoniously combines contemporary elements with traditional motifs.

The low profile, detached console, with its eight level memory system and touch plate controls, affords the player/director convenience and balance.

The success of this project was due, not only to the variety of materials and developments in technology, but more so to the talents, ideas and dedication of the many people at St. Rita's Parish and Steiner-Reck, Inc.

St. Rita's Church has an organ of which to be proud. We hope it will be a source of inspiration to all . . . listeners, organists, and composers.

— *Gottfried C. Reck*

St. Rita Church's Steiner-Reck pipe organ specifications, by Gottfried C. Reck. *Paul Skevington.*

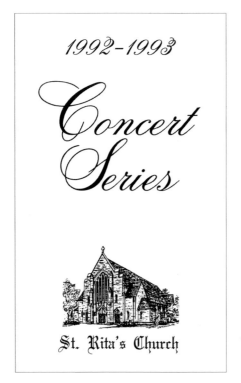

1992-1993

Concert Series

St. Rita's Church

The Steiner-Reck pipe organ inspired an early 1990s concert and recital series at St. Rita Church. *Paul Skevington.*

On May 1, 1990, St. Rita Parish officially dedicated its new Steiner-Reck organ among more than 350 attendees who gathered at the church for a hymn celebration led by Dr. Paul Skevington with the St. Rita Church choir. The parish soon held frequent organ, trumpet, and brass recitals and concert series at the church. Dr. Skevington remained as St. Rita Parish's music director and organist from 1987 until 1993, when he joined Father McGuill at St. Luke Parish in McLean, Virginia, as its director of music and director of RCIA.

A NEW GENERATION OF THE FAITHFUL

In the late 1980s and early 1990s, the Del Ray and Potomac Yard sections of Alexandria began to attract a growing number of young singles, married couples, and families. Many of them became part of a new generation of the Catholic faithful who began to revitalize an aging St. Rita Parish through their engagement in the parish community. As much as they admired the physical beauty of St. Rita Church, they were also inspired by Father

Above: Members of the St. Rita Church choir, circa late 1980s. *Paul Skevington.*

Left: Father Mark Moretti, St. Rita Parish associate pastor, circa late 1990s. *St. Rita Parish Archives.*

ST. RITA'S GRAPEVINE

Summer 1997 | VOLUME 2, ISSUE 4

HOME AND SCHOOL ASSOCIATION UPDATE

By Don and Kathy Campbell

You can see the smiles on our kids' faces as the school year comes to a close. Just ahead lies a summer filled with fun and relaxation — but before we say goodbye until the fall, we wanted to say thanks to all the teachers, faculty and parents who make Saint Rita's so special. We are blessed to have such a special group to guide our children as they grow physically, mentally and spiritually. We will remember this year's school theme of the "Giving Tree". Let us all continue to offer unconditional love to our children as they uncover life's adventures.

The 1996-97 school year was another wonderful experience. We had two great socials; our ice cream social at Halloween and our sock hop at Valentine's. Boy, do Saint Rita's families know how to eat and dance!

During the school year, the children learned new ideas and skills and enjoyed their field trips. Through the efforts of some great families, we earned a healthy profit through our fall wrapping paper fundraiser, our spring fundraiser selling success cards and the Del Ray Farmer's Market bake sales. We plan to do even better next year so we can enhance the schools curriculum and provide our teachers with the little things that make a difference.

We thoroughly enjoyed our two years as co-presidents and are pleased to pass the baton on to our new officers. Judy Meiklejohn will take over as president, with Rosemary Lynch as her vice. Genevieve Heisley remains as treasurer and our new secretary is Cheryll Brillhart. We will remain in close touch, as we hope you will. Parent participation is what makes our school so special.

On behalf of the Home and School Board, have a joyful summer and we'll see you in September.

SCHOOL HONORS SENIOR VOLUNTEERS

Five of Saint Rita's unsung heroes were honored at the second annual Justin D. McClunn Society Banquet at the Sheraton Premier in Tysons Corner on May 4. Mr. Cyril Malloy, Mr. Frank Powers, Mr. Wilbur Gorham and Mr. Victor Baran received certificates of appreciation and were hosted at the dinner by the Home and School Association. Also honored posthumously was Mr. Len Dolan who died last year.

"For many, many years these men have spent each Tuesday making needed repairs to the school and convent," said Sister Catherine. "They've done it all, from paint-

continued on page 2

Christ is the reason for this school. He is the unseen but ever present Teacher in its classes, the Model for its faculty, the Inspiration for its students.

One way to share information was St. Rita's Home and School Association's *The Grapevine* newsletter, 1997. *Maureen Schweers.*

O'Hara's humanity and Father McGuill's compassion and charity. They joined parish groups, such as the church choir and a parent cooperative childcare group held in the parish center during Sunday Mass, in which they befriended a wide spectrum of fellow parishioners.

These parishioners' love for their new spiritual home translated into charitable works with lasting impact, such as the establishment of a home-mothers' children's play group that formed long-term friendships rooted in faith, active involvement in the Saint Rita School Home and School Association, and years of steady stewardship of St. Rita Church's altar servers. During these years of further growth, these newcomers seized countless other opportunities to serve the St. Rita Parish and School community and discovered the ways of Providence guiding them and building up God's kingdom. Another former St. Rita parishioner and alumnus would join them in the 1990s, Father Mark Moretti, who would serve as parochial vicar. A graduate of St. Rita School, Bishop Ireton High School, and Allentown College of St. Francis de Sales (now DeSales University), he was also a world-traveled former U.S. State Department special agent. Father Moretti's solid faith formation, international perspective, and administrative skills suited him well in assisting the St. Rita community's growth in grace and wisdom.

A New St. Rita School Principal

St. Francis de Sales once wrote, "We all have a vocation. We believe that God has placed us in this life to fill a special need that no one else can accomplish." In 1998, Mrs. Mary Pat Schlickenmaier's calling to youth education placed her in a position to fill a particularly important need at St. Rita School. She had studied pre-medical school courses in college, taught at a high school, and, since 1985, taught science at her grade school alma mater, St. Mary Catholic School in Alexandria. With the encouragement of family and friends, she placed her trust in God and applied for the principal position at St. Rita School. The process was somewhat grueling—at least thirteen people interviewed her about the position. Nonetheless, while walking around the school after the interviews were done, she sensed that God had placed her precisely where He needed her to be. Her sense was confirmed when she was offered the St. Rita School principal position.

Mrs. Schlickenmaier—known to all as simply "Mrs. S."—was the school's first principal who was not a religious Sister, and she would serve in the position from 1998 to 2019. Of course, she did all this with the help of the Sisters of St. Joseph at the school. Especially during her earliest years as principal, Sister Frances Amata was in Mrs. Schlickenmaier's words the

Above: The St. Rita of Cascia statue at St. Rita School. *Centennial History Subcommittee.*

Opposite: The IBM Selectric II typewriter, which was perpetually used by the Sisters of St. Joseph at the school. *St. Rita School Archives.*

"heart and soul" of the school through her humble service, including acting as her secretary.

By 1998, the school consisted of fifteen teachers, including two Sisters of St. Joseph. It had a diverse student population of about two hundred students with fifty students from Bolling Air Force Base. The curriculum included foreign language courses and a strong focus on science and computer labs. A full-time librarian staffed a large library, and remedial reading specialists were available to students.

Mrs. Schlickenmaier looked for ways to improve and beautify the school. In 1999, she traveled to the Shrine of St. Rita of Cascia in Philadelphia, Pennsylvania, where she discovered a beautiful, yet expensive, statue of the patron saint of impossible causes. In St. Rita Parish's tradition of "doing the impossible," a kind and generous benefactor made possible the acquisition of the statue, and Mr. and Mrs. Schlickenmaier drove to Philadelphia in a sport utility vehicle to bring St. Rita to her namesake parish in Alexandria. The statue remained inside the school for several months until it was set in its current location among rose and azalea bushes on the west side of the school along Russell Road. St. Rita was thus there permanently in stone, watching over and protecting school and parish as a new millennium beckoned.

ENTERING THE NEW MILLENNIUM, 2000–2010

A Pastor for the New Millennium

With the new millennium came a new pastor. Father Denis Donahue arrived at St. Rita in June 2000. It was his first time as a pastor, and his journey to the parish had been remarkable. As a young teenager, he was shot twice by a sniper in a random, terrible act of violence in his Ann Arbor, Michigan neighborhood while delivering papers. After multiple surgeries, and after his parents were told that he would not survive, he did recover, albeit with permanent physical disabilities. He learned to walk again, and later, as he described it, he truly began to feel the presence of Christ in his life. Ultimately, Christ led him to the priesthood.

Father Donahue came to St. Rita with a sense of mission and dedication. He realized the great responsibility that rested on him as pastor. He noted the decline in student enrollment due to changing demographics and other factors, and he was aware that tuition costs made it difficult for local Spanish-speaking children to attend. Over the next decade, he worked closely with Mrs. Schlickenmaier to spearhead a remarkable school renaissance.

Father Donahue was also the first specially designated bilingual pastor, allowing him to minister more fully to the local Spanish-speaking community. Fortunately, he had a dedicated group of Spanish-speaking community leaders such as Angela Reyes to assist him. He helped develop a Hispanic Legion of Mary, and he established a Hispanic youth group to provide a good, clean environment for local boys and girls to meet and to socialize.

Mrs. Mary Pat Schlickenmaier, principal, and Father Denis Donahue, pastor. *Mary Pat Schlickenmaier.*

The Spanish-speaking community's own special charism and devotion were especially evident during Father Donahue's years as pastor. As one example, on Good Friday 2007, Father Donahue and Marlene Orellana, head of the Hispanic diocesan Pastoral Institute, helped to lead a *Via Crucis*, a way of the cross *en vivo* (a living Way of the Cross). This custom, which had arrived long ago from Spain to Latin America, brought to life Jesus's suffering and death in vivid form, as participants gathered and reenacted the Lord's road to Calvary.

Additionally, Father Donahue initiated many devotional practices, including prayers and novenas to the parish patroness herself that were offered to implore her intercession. He established Eucharistic Adoration time for the students at the school on Fridays, so the children could go into the church and stay for a time and adore the Lord in the Blessed Sacrament. During that time, they would hear from Father Donahue and other priests and learned to pray better and to meditate on Jesus's love for them.

Such devotional practices undergirded practical action. Father Donahue tirelessly worked to improve the church and surrounding campus, and his

This page, top: A re-creation of the Via Crucis. *From the* Arlington Catholic Herald.

This page, bottom: Alberto and Nina Bacani. *From the* Arlington Catholic Herald.

Opposite: Lawrence Bowie, St. Rita director of music. *Lawrence Bowie.*

fervor clearly paid off. In one instance, Father Donahue recalled having concerns about the parish debt. Those concerns were answered by the generosity of someone who was not even a member of St. Rita Parish, but of the nearby parish of Our Lady of Lourdes. The benefactor provided a $1.6 million gift that erased much if not all the parish debt, all at once!

Other projects ensued. Father Donahue upgraded the parish center. Parishioners Chris Hart and Carlos Olvera organized a series of parish picnics beginning in 2004, with a goal bringing together the English- and Spanish-speaking communities. And while the influx of youth was widely

noted, lifelong fidelity and faithfulness were also recognized. As one example, in June 2007, parishioners Alberto and Nina Bacani, both in their nineties, renewed their marriage vows in the presence of Father Donahue, along with their children, grandchildren, and great-grandchildren. As Alberto said, "The necessity of building a marriage on one's faith is paramount." From their first meeting in the Philippines, through World War II, through the loss of two of their five children to cancer, and through all other hardships, their seventy-year marriage was a shining testament and an ideal to aspire to for the younger generation.

An emphasis was also made on the musical treasures of the church. In 2001, Father Donahue hired Lawrence Bowie to serve as the parish organist, and in a few years, he also became the director of music. Mr. Bowie, who had previously served as director of music and organist at the Cathedral of St. Mary in Peoria, Illinois, brought immense musical knowledge and ability. He gradually introduced sung propers, Gregorian psalm tones, and Latin motets to the Masses and thereby revealed the priceless treasure of the church's liturgical music to a new generation of faithful. In more than twenty years as director of music, Mr. Bowie has continued to provide exceptional sacred music for countless Masses and other services, with the goal of lifting the hearts and minds of all to God.

TRAGEDY AND PERSEVERANCE

The early 2000s was a time of growth and possibility, but it was also a time of turmoil, tragedy, and suffering. Of course, the entire nation was shocked and horrified by the cataclysmic events of September 11, 2001, when terrorists hijacked and crashed airliners across the eastern United States. Thousands were murdered at the World Trade Center, in a plane that crashed on a desolate field in Pennsylvania, and just three and a half miles north of St.

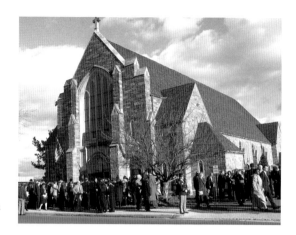

Outside the funeral of Nancy Dunning, December 2003. *From the* Arlington Catholic Herald.

Rita at the Pentagon. Father Donahue recalled that he offered Mass at around 3:00 p.m. in the school hall for any children and teachers who were still there. Amid the heartbreak and confusion, it was necessary to turn to God with the most powerful prayer that could be offered.

The parish also was profoundly affected by a terrible, more intimate tragedy that occurred two years later, in late 2003, when Nancy Dunning, wife of Alexandria sheriff James Dunning, was murdered at her home in the nearby neighborhood in a senseless act of violence. Although she was a registered parishioner of Blessed Sacrament Church, she frequently attended Mass at St. Rita. Her funeral Mass, at St. Rita, was attended by nearly one thousand people, and Father Donahue and Father John Cregan, pastor at Blessed Sacrament, concelebrated. In the words of Dunning family friend Jesuit Father James Walsh, her "life was a gift…and as the past recedes, we will feel her life as a gift."

The School Welcomes in the Twenty-First Century

While parish life seemed to come alive in the new century, the school also built and expanded on on what had come before. Mrs. Schlickenmaier noted that her first few years at the school had often been "improvisational," as she and others, particularly Sister Frances Amata, performed any number of tasks that went far beyond "just" being principal. Needing doors for the school's classrooms, for example, the principal found perfectly good doors that had been thrown out by a local public school. She obtained them for free and put them to good use. Enrollment by the end of the 1990s and early 2000s had reduced to about 160 students, but Mrs. S., Father Donahue, and the committed teachers and staff at St. Rita were not perturbed. They would, with God's help and their patroness's intercession, persevere and prevail.

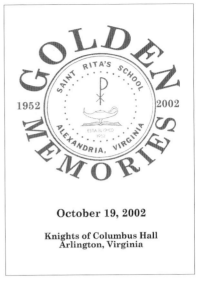

In 2002, the school celebrated its golden anniversary, and many alumni from days past reminisced fondly. The school's Golden Memories Reunion Committee made possible a series of events over an October weekend that included an ice cream social, a reception and dance, and a commemorative

The Golden Memories Book for the fiftieth anniversary of St. Rita School, October 2002. *St. Rita School Archives.*

Mass. The event was a wonderful success, as alumni reminisced about the "days of old."

But the future also beckoned, and the school's principal was indefatigable in her efforts to bring the school to it. To ensure the school's viability, which included boosting enrollment, she worked closely with what was known as the Metro School Diocesan Consortium to come up with ideas and to further efforts to obtain financial assistance and increase awareness about the school.

A cascade of ideas, projects, activities, and events followed. Mrs. Schlickenmaier helped design the new school logo and developed its motto, *Pax per sapientiam* ("Peace through wisdom"), as well as the school's byline taken from Pope Pius XI: "The soul of education is the education of the soul." In 2004, the first St. Rita School 5K race was run. It would become a community event lasting to the present day that raises tens of thousands of dollars and brings in hundreds of runners from across the region. A walk for the homeless by the schoolchildren (typically on All Saints' Day) became a tradition to draw attention to the least cared for in the community. A school auction began as well—the first was held to raise money for a school copier that cost $7,000. That auction now is the school's premier annual fundraising event, with generous benefactors from across the region. An extended

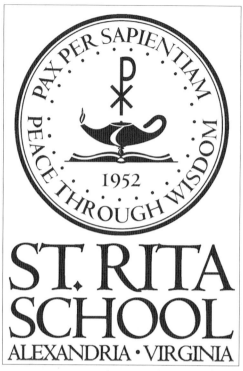

Left: The St. Rita logo. *St. Rita School Archives.*

Below: A St. Rita School Walk for the Homeless. *Mary Pat Schlickenmaier.*

Opposite, top: The St. Rita School 5K has become an annual tradition. *Mary Pat Schlickenmaier.*

Opposite, bottom: The St. Rita School auction is another annual tradition. *Elizabeth Fitton.*

Above: Letting the good times roll at a recent St. Rita School Auction. *Elizabeth Fitton.*

Opposite, top: Some of the winners of the annual Beiro Awards. *Mary Pat Schlickenmaier.*

Opposite, bottom: Josephine Cunningham and Cindy Hart, two school mainstays. *Mary Pat Schlickenmaier.*

day program was started before and after school to allow working parents a safe, secure, and faith-filled environment for their children. And not to be forgotten was the work of the Tuesday men—retired gentlemen of the parish who would meet on Tuesdays at the church, have coffee, and then do whatever handyman jobs were needed at the school.

Meanwhile, there were a number of initiatives within the school walls as well. A school play was established, as were spelling and geography bees. A strings group—the first in the diocese—was founded. A kindly benefactor asked Mrs. Schlickenmaier how much was needed for a new science lab. She promptly responded, "$50,000." The benefactor provided exactly that. The Beiro family, community stalwarts, and longtime parishioners, established a scholarship fund for St. Rita students (and for students at other diocesan schools). In 2006, the family also provided an award for an annual essay writing contest, which continues to be awarded to this day.

Around this time, one interested parent, Josephine Cunningham, noted how open, accessible, and kindhearted those at the school were. She ended up not only enrolling her children at St. Rita but also later became an integral volunteer member of the Parent-Teacher Organization (PTO) and eventually served for many years as director of admissions.

The St. Rita School playground being built. *Mary Pat Schlickenmaier.*

If there was any single event that crystallized the energy, faithfulness, and community spirit of the school during the early 2000s, it was the surely the building of the school playground. Parishioner and school parent Cindy Hart, along with other parents and Mrs. Schlickenmaier, had noted the lack of a designated space for the children to play on the school grounds. After consultation with the Sisters about the yard area just outside the adjoining convent, the decision was made to build the playground there. What the school lacked in funding for that project, it made up for in spirit, sweat, and "amateur" expertise. And so, one weekend in 2005, there occurred what parishioner Chris Durel said was something akin to a "barn raising." Parents—especially the fathers—came in over the weekend and worked shifts all through the day, with Father Donahue and Mrs. Schlickenmaier beside them. All day and night they worked, with the project being completed and blessed by Father Donahue that Sunday. The building of the playground was, as Mrs. Schlickenmaier. recalled, a catalyzing event. It signified that with prayer, hard work, and trust, opportunities could be had and major goals could be attained.

Rebuilding and Revival

Father Paul Scalia arrived at St. Rita in 2004 to serve as parochial vicar, his third priestly assignment. Father Scalia, like so many St. Rita priests, had grown up in the Diocese of Arlington. He was from a large family, and his father was U.S. Supreme Court justice Antonin Scalia. He studied theology at the Pontifical Gregorian University and the Pontifical University of Saint Thomas Aquinas in Rome. He was—and is—a noted, prolific author as well as a renowned speaker and homilist. He was immediately struck by several things at St. Rita: the fraternal atmosphere in the rectory, the camaraderie among the teachers, and the beauty of the church structure itself. Noting the church's simple, stately beauty, he recalled, "It stirred me."

Father Scalia further noted the changing demographics of the parish. Along with an increased and increasingly vibrant Spanish-speaking community, there also came a decided youthfulness in the parish. He noted how young couples seemed to shift over to the parish, while the older cohort who had resided nearby, and who had been parishioners and students in the first postwar decades of the past century, had largely moved on. Much of the good work that had been done by that generation needed refurbishment. Father Scalia especially noted how Father Donahue placed a great deal of emphasis on improving the physical plant and parts of the church and school campus area. Nature's own course only added to the need for repair and improvement. Father Scalia even recalled how water

Father Paul Scalia with St. Rita schoolchildren. *From the* Arlington Catholic Herald.

flooded from Four Mile Run and ran all the way up to Russell Road and to the doorstep of the church itself.

Amid all this change, it was Father Scalia who reinstituted the Traditional Latin Mass at St. Rita, after the publication of Pope Benedict XVI's motu proprio *Summorum Pontificum* in 2007, which encouraged reintroduction of the ancient liturgy. He began that same year on the Feast of St. Michael, September 29, and subsequently offered a Requiem High Mass that November. Masses were offered from then on by Father Scalia as occasions arose. And in reintroducing it, he made sure that its context and meaning were made known. Not only were St. Rita altar boys appropriately trained, but Father also provided instruction on the venerable rite to the faithful. The seeds were thus planted for a more complete integration of the Traditional Latin Mass in the next decade.

A Deacon for St. Rita

Deacon Stephen Dixon has another name—he is also known as "Mr. St. Rita." He has been a lifelong parishioner—in fact, he was part of the first first-grade class at the school when it opened its doors in 1952. After attending all eight years there, when he also served on the altar and sang in the choir, he went to minor seminary (the now closed St. John Vianney Minor Seminary in Richmond) for a year. In his own words, at that time, he "didn't get the call" and instead came back and finished high school in Alexandria. There he met his future wife, Thana. They dated in high school and college, were married in 1969, and had twin daughters Donna and Debbie the following year.

He and his family were parishioners during those years as well. He served as a lector and cantor, and over time, he felt the calling to serve even more. His road to the diaconate began somewhat spontaneously. Fathers Donahue and Moretti asked him if he had ever considered being a deacon. He had never really considered it, but Bishop Paul Loverde had recently reinstituted the permanent diaconate in the diocese, which had been reintroduced by Pope Paul VI after the Second Vatican Council. As opposed to a transitional deacon, who expects to be ordained as a priest, a permanent deacon does not. Married men may thus be ordained deacons.

Mr. Dixon began the program in 2006, along with nineteen other men in the diocese. He recalled going every Saturday over a five-year period

Deacon Stephen Dixon blessing throats on St. Blaise's Day. *Mary Pat Schlickenmaier.*

to Paul VI High School in Fairfax, where he and the other candidates underwent extensive training. Ultimately, in 2011, he was ordained and immediately began service at St. Rita as its first permanent deacon. Sadly, his beloved wife, Thana, died in 2016, but his daughters and their families are still parishioners, with Debbie also as the parish business manager. Deacon Dixon ministers in any and all sorts of ways in the parish. He helps with marriage preparation, performs baptisms, presides at benedictions and during holy hours, leads rosaries, preaches from the pulpit, helps with the hospital ministry, and performs any number of blessings. In both his lifelong association with the parish and his continued service, the deacon has truly earned the title "Mr. St. Rita."

ST. RITA TODAY AND TOMORROW, 2010–PRESENT

Introducing Father Gee

Father Daniel Gee became the pastor of St. Rita in 2010, and he very much looked to continue and to further the work of Father Donahue. A navy "brat" who had spent much of his youth in the Arlington diocese, he attended the University of Oregon, where he majored in Spanish. After the seminary, Father Gee also spent time in the Dominican Republic, where he did mission work and perfected his Spanish language skills. And just as his predecessor did, he put those skills to use to serve the parish's vibrant, growing Spanish-speaking community. He had other talents. He was an avid cyclist and runner—he could be frequently seen biking the neighborhood, and he ran the annual St. Rita 5K race at competitive speeds. He also taught boxing to the boys in the upper school grades. His abilities branched out further—a skilled guitarist, he sometimes played, with other parishioners and seminarians, at St. Rita festival days and other events. He even served as the auctioneer at the annual school auctions. He was joined in the parish by Father Vincent Bork, who would serve as the parochial vicar throughout the 2010s. Father Bork brought his own talents: he was a trained scientist, with a PhD in physics. Both were dedicated to God and to the St. Rita faithful.

Much was accomplished while Father Gee served as pastor. A homeschooling group was founded in 2014 to integrate homeschool children and their families into both parish and school life. Homeschool children now regularly participate in school athletics, school plays, and any

Left: Father Daniel Gee, St. Rita pastor, offering Mass. *From the* Arlington Catholic Herald.

Below: St. Rita Men's Group about to go on an early morning ruck march. *From the* Arlington Catholic Herald.

St. Rita Young Adult Group Harper's Ferry outing. *Nicholas Barrow.*

American Heritage Girls at the Alexandria National Cemetery. *Maureen Schweers.*

number of other school activities, and they also receive catechesis and sacramental preparation. The Legion of Mary became a fixture in the parish, and currently there are active English- and Spanish-speaking *praesidia*, as well as a Junior Legion of Mary for school and parish children. Legionnaires perform spiritual works of mercy in the community, including visits to residences and senior homes. The Knights of Columbus became officially established as a St. Rita Council, and they provided a number of services to the parish and community. Also, a St. Rita Young Adult Group was established for the young adults to meet and to socialize.

Organizations were started for school-age children as well. American Heritage Girls Troop VA 1381—with the troop number marking St. Rita's birth year—was established at St. Rita in 2012. The girls participate in various activities, badge programs, outdoor adventures, and service projects to benefit the parish and the community at large. In 2018, four fathers met in 2018 to discuss establishing a Catholic-oriented group for boys, and after much hard work, in March 2022, Troop of St. George 552 was established for the young men of the parish to engage in a faith-oriented "apostolate of adventure" grounded in virtue.

A Preschool Is Founded

Early in his tenure as pastor, Father Gee, with Mrs. Schlickenmaier's able assistance, determined to establish a preschool. Changing demographics, such as the arrival of many young families, helped prompt the decision. Utilizing the parish hall building (which had formerly been the upper school for grades six through eight), the preschool opened in the fall of 2011, after being blessed by Bishop Paul Loverde.

St. Rita Preschool is a play-based environment where children learn to develop mentally, emotionally, and spiritually. It includes incorporating the teaching methods first developed by Catholic educator Maria Montessori. The preschool has a program for two- and three-year-olds (called Angels), three- and four-year-olds (Lambs), and four- and five-year-olds (Shepherds).

The teachers at the preschool take a committed "hands-on" approach, and children not only learn but also reach out and touch the incarnate truths of the Catholic faith. Each week, children step out of the play-based classroom and step into the atrium, which is part of the Montessori-based Catechesis of the Good Shepherd (CGS). In the atrium, children handle statues and

Bishop Loverde Blesses the St. Rita Preschool. *Mary Pat Schlickenmaier.*

St. Rita Preschool children. *St. Rita School Archives.*

hold figures of our Lord, the Blessed Mother, and the saints. They learn various activities (called "works") at model altars or baptismal fonts. Further, in accordance with Montessori techniques, children learn prayer, problem solving, and emergent reading and writing. The CGS program has become such a part of the St. Rita way of thinking that Level 2 CGS is now provided for children up to third grade at the school. Mrs. Caitlin Rockwell, who came on staff in 2012, eventually took over as full-time director in 2016, and under her leadership, the preschool continues to grow and thrive.

The School Flourishes and a Classical Curriculum Is Established

The school continued to flourish in the 2010s. The student body grew in numbers. Teachers and faculty worked tirelessly, including some Sisters of St. Joseph, who continued to provide quality, close-up education. Events such as the annual five-kilometer race and auction that began in the early to mid-2000s had, by the 2010s, became regular significant school and community events. The 5K race drew in hundreds of runners not only from the parish and local community but also even beyond, with competitive racers now participating and with local businesses donating generously. The annual auction, usually held just before Lent, brought in sponsors from across Northern Virginia and even farther, with out-of-state and international trips among the many things auctioned off (including delicious baked goods from students and families). In addition to these annual fundraisers, students continued to be active in the many field trips, CYO and athletic opportunities, and the annual school plays, all of which attested to the vibrancy of St. Rita School.

The curriculum also significantly developed. After having firmly established the preschool, Mrs. Schlickenmaier and Father Gee began to discuss finding better ways to have an integrated course of study that brought together history, literature, art, music, mathematics, science, and the teachings of the Catholic faith. The goal was to build up rounded, well-educated, and fully developed students. They determined that education in the classical tradition—which utilized an integrated understanding of the ancient, medieval, early modern, and modern periods—would be the approach best suited to illuminate student minds.

This page, top: Sister Alma, SSJ, and Sister Terry, SSJ. *Mary Pat Schlickenmaier.*

This page, bottom: The St. Rita School 5K continues as a major community event. *St. Rita School Archives.*

Opposite: St. Rita schoolchildren take a bow after a performance of *The Wizard of Oz*, 2019. *Mary Pat Schlickenmaier.*

The program fully began in 2017. Teachers were trained in the method and were encouraged to develop their lessons using primary sources more than textbooks. They began to use truth, beauty, and goodness as a transcendental lens through which to see all of God's creation as well as His hand in history. After Mrs. Schlickenmaier's retirement in 2019, the COVID-19 pandemic put the program on hold. However, it is now back on course, and the school is proud to provide the classical teaching method in a parochial context. At St. Rita School, the classical model utilizes repetition of themes over the course of one's time at the school, providing a deeper and fuller look on the second cycle. This means that first graders are introduced to the ancient worlds of Egypt, Greece, and Rome and will return to these themes in the fifth grade. Sixth graders study the Renaissance and Reformation periods, having done so previously in the second grade. Third and seventh graders look at early modern history, and fourth and eighth grades study modern history. These first two cycles correspond to the first two levels of the trivium (grammar and logic), and they would most ideally be completed with a third cycle (rhetoric), which would normally happen during the high school years. A great benefit to the classical approach is to tie students' learning to their developmental stages and to teach ways that fully engage their minds, bodies, and souls.

The Traditional Latin Mass on Sundays

The Traditional Latin Mass had already been reestablished at St. Rita, primarily due to the work of parochial vicar Father Paul Scalia in the 2000s. Gradually, the venerable rite came to be celebrated on Tuesday and Thursday evenings, in its Low Mass form, by Father Gee and Father Bork. In early 2017, Father Gee decided, on an experimental basis, to provide a Traditional Latin Mass once a month on Sundays as well. The experiment quickly became a success. Longtime devotees of the traditional liturgy, as well as younger faithful, made it quite a popular choice. As a result, in May of that year, the Mass began to be offered every Sunday morning. Since then, the numbers of faithful who attend the Mass have significantly increased, with weekly Sunday attendance close to four hundred.

Left: The Traditional Latin Mass returned on Sundays in 2017 and is very popular. *Centennial History Subcommittee.*

Opposite: Another view of the very popular Traditional Latin Mass. *Ryan Ellis.*

Furthermore, the introduction on Sunday, and deeper integration into parish life, of the Traditional Latin Mass has been accompanied by a corresponding deeper overall devotion and fervor throughout the parish. Attendees of the older rite are full members of the St. Rita community and participate totally in parish activities, committees, and school organizations.

Unity, charity, and mutual respect are parish watchwords, as St. Rita has fully and successfully become "trilingual," with Sunday Masses in English, Spanish, and Latin.

The Spanish-Speaking Community's Continued Growth

The Spanish-speaking parish community continued to grow during the 2010s and early 2020s, and it has further enriched the parish in several ways. For example, each year, to begin the Spanish Palm Sunday Mass, members of the community have dressed as disciples and women of Jerusalem as they process into the church. Later that week, on Good Friday, the Living Stations of the Cross has been a well-attended and popular event. The organizers spend all of Lent planning and practicing, and just before the Spanish Good Friday Service of the Lord's Passion, they reenact the last steps of our Lord before His death. On December 12, the Feast of Our Lady of Guadalupe is especially joyously celebrated, with a replica of Our Lady's tilma lovingly decorated in the sanctuary. And there is also the enactment during Advent of *Los Posadas* ("Shelter") to commemorate the journey of Joseph and Mary from Nazareth to Jerusalem and their search of lodging—with scripture and spiritual works being read at each stop.

Opposite: Father Gee presiding at a Palm Sunday Procession. *From the* Arlington Catholic Herald.

Above: Our Lady of Guadalupe honored on her feast day, December 12. *Mary Pat Schlickenmaier.*

International Assistance

As the demand for Sacraments increased with an influx of more parishioners, Father Gee saw another avenue to utilize for support. Priests from Poland studying in Washington, D.C., needed a parish to live in and St. Rita filled that requirement. The first Polish resident priest was Father Marcin Krycki, who arrived in 2012. He left in 2015, and Father Karol Nedza from the Diocese of Sosnowiec came to replace him. When Father Nedza completed his studies and returned to Poland, Father Łukasz Duda from the Archdiocese of Warsaw stepped in. After three years of studying and enjoying life at St. Rita, he returned to Poland in June 2024. These priests have been of great service to the parish, and it is hoped that more can follow!

The Parish's "Littlest Saints"

It is a pious and ancient tradition of the Catholic Church that local saints are often buried on the grounds of a parish, where they can be venerated and asked for intercession. It is also a truth of the faith that baptized children who die at an early age are indeed saints—already cleansed of original sin, they leave the world with no other sins, and thus have no need of Purgatory's refining fire.

In early 2017, two-year-old Everett Doerrer, son of St. Rita parishioners Paul and Leigha Doerrer, had an unexpected seizure. After his parents rushed

The graves of St. Everett and St. Maria Therese of Alexandria. *Centennial History Subcommittee.*

him to the hospital, a full day passed as valiant efforts to revive Everett were undertaken. Leigha described them as "24 hours of mercies" that allowed her and Paul to prepare for the worst. When all efforts failed, Father Bork was there to say prayers and confirm little Everett. While Leigha held him in her arms, Everett died.

Because he died in the fullness of grace, he is now St. Everett of Alexandria. Shortly after Everett's passing, Father Gee celebrated the funeral Mass of the Angels. There is no need now to pray *for* Everett—he is among the angels and can be prayed *to*. And with his family's approval, St. Everett's grave is now located just outside the church. He is joined by another saint of the parish, St. Maria Therese Ledbetter, who died just a few months after her birth in 2021. At this "Shrine of the Holy Innocents," miscarried infants are also buried, and here the faithful can find solace and seek the help and intercession of the parish's "littlest saints."

Helping Those in Need in the Community

People at St. Rita have for years been helping those in the local community in any number of ways. Longtime parishioners such as Susanne Arnold have been well known for spearheading the St. Rita social outreach program and for providing food and clothing and for working with the

The Mother of Light Center in action. *Mother of Light Center.*

parish to help locals with matters such as paying electric and gas bills via the St. Rita Help Line.

Two events helped to further social outreach. In 2018, the parish purchased a small house across from the school on Glebe Road and named it the Casita Santa Rita. It has since become a place to hold small meetings and to have clothing drives in the fall and spring. In the following year, another major Catholic organization was established in the local area, with the full support of St. Rita Parish. The Mother of Light Center, located one mile away from the church on Clifford Avenue, provides for the needy of the area. Its mission statement says that its purpose is to "uplift the impoverished, destitute, and homeless men and women in our local community, aiding them in constructing lives imbued with stability, purpose, and hope—all for the greater glory of God and the salvation of souls." Many St. Rita parishioners are involved with the center, and in recent years, the relationship between the center and the parish has deepened. Anniversary celebrations for the center have been held in the parish hall, and Mother of Light Center summer camps have been held on parish and school grounds.

COVID-19: Its Consequences
and the St. Rita Response

In 2020, the COVID-19 pandemic spread across the world. St. Rita Parish and School did not escape its impact, but parish and school persevered amid challenges and difficulties. Trust in God and reliance on the parish patroness's protection undergirded prudent, thoughtful action on the part of clergy, faculty, and faithful families and parishioners. Extreme positions were avoided, and safe, continuous access to the Sacraments and education were provided.

In early spring of 2020, the governor of Virginia ordered the closure of all schools in the state. St. Rita School began its own version of "online" learning for the remainder of that school year, largely through the tireless efforts of faculty and staff, led by Principal Mrs. Melissa Manaker, who had succeeded Mrs. Schlickenmaier in 2019. While this was a best possible short-term solution, faculty, staff, and clergy all agreed that such online learning, especially for young children, was far short of ideal.

Mrs. Bethany Hamm, who had worked as both a lawyer and educator and who had worked on establishing school procedures and protocols in the past, noted the difficulty with her own children enrolled at St. Rita. Working with education officials and health experts, Mrs. Hamm and other members of the St. Rita faculty drafted plans that would allow the school to reopen in the fall of 2020. Father Gee was also directly involved: he wanted, while always following health and safety requirements, to create as normal a learning experience as possible for the St. Rita schoolchildren.

The school did indeed reopen in the fall of 2020. It was a tumultuous period for faculty, staff, students, and parents. As Mrs. Hamm remembered, emotions ran high. There was much anxiety, as little was known about the

St. Rita School during COVID, 2020. *St. Rita School Archive.*

pandemic. Safety was paramount. Air purifiers were set up in each classroom. Rigorous reporting requirements were established to report any outbreak of COVID among students. School classrooms were divided to provide spacing, and teachers had to instruct separate students in different rooms twice each day. While such efforts were inspiring and heroic, the teachers ended their days often physically, mentally, and emotionally weary.

In the words of Mrs. Hamm, who had assumed the duties of principal in the fall of 2020, the experience "stripped things down to the essential" in learning. It reminded everyone of the important things—first and foremost, to continue to instill in the children the truth of the Catholic faith, to always treat others with kindness and charity, and to focus on the education fundamentals.

Meanwhile, Fathers Gee and Bork worked mightily to continue to provide priestly care and the Sacraments to the faithful. Public Masses ceased after March 16, 2020, and St. Rita, like many other churches, provided Sunday Mass online. Soon afterward, outdoor Sunday Eucharistic services were briefly held for a few weeks in late spring. All the while during the shutdown, the St. Rita priests faithfully offered private

Mass daily on behalf of the parish for the glory of God. As soon as possible, the Holy Sacrifice of the Mass was restored to the church, with a decided twist. While many church doors were shut, the fathers of St. Rita did the opposite. To both ensure the safety of their parishioners and to provide them access to the Sacraments, the fathers *doubled* the number of Sunday Masses. The faithful were distanced, with green ribbons blocking alternate rows and blue crosses taped to the Communion rail to ensure distancing. Thus, half the normal number could attend each Mass, but during this time Masses in English, Latin, and Spanish were said virtually on the hour, every hour, on Sundays.

The result of all this prudent planning and action—all with the support of the diocese and Bishop Burbidge and never out of step with local requirements—was a continuation of education, sacramental grace, and continued fellowship. No significant outbreak of COVID was ever reported in either church or school.

A New Decade and a New Pastor: Father Christensen

In June 2021, a new pastor came to St. Rita. Father Christopher Christensen, a relatively young pastor only a few years out of the seminary, nonetheless came well prepared. Father Christensen was a Notre Dame graduate, where he had majored in philosophy and Japanese (like Father Gee, he was a military brat and had spent some of his youth in Japan when his father was stationed there). He had also served as a navy surface warfare office prior to entering the seminary. Something of a linguist, he (in his own words) "picked up" Spanish while taking classes at the seminary, later improved his use of the language while working in Guatemala during a seminary summer session, and then refined it while serving at St. John the Apostle in Leesburg with the large Spanish-speaking community there. While working on Spanish, he also learned how to offer the Traditional Latin Mass.

In his assignment at the cathedral, Father Christensen noticed how young couples he saw there seemed to end up at St. Rita. When later assigned as the St. Rita pastor, he was welcomed at the parish by Father Nicholas Schierer, who had in 2020 replaced Father Bork as parochial vicar. Father Schierer, who grew up in nearby Herndon (and whose brother is also a priest), brought his own special talents, not the least of which includes his extraordinary

Father Christopher Christensen greets parishioners. *From the* Arlington Catholic Herald.

skills at cooking and grilling. He can frequently be seen presiding over a grill station at any number of parish and school events.

Together, they continue to carry on and further the work of their priestly predecessors. Many developments have occurred since their arrival. Inspectors informed the school that the playground needed to be significantly upgraded. School parent Johnny Taylor provided the funding, and in 2023, a beautiful new playground was built, continuing the loving legacy of the one built nearly two decades before. A security fence was added to protect the children while at school. Given the overflow of congregants, the nearby, nationally famous Birchmere Music Hall now provides Sunday parking space. An annual St. Nicholas Market was established, bringing together parishioners, members of the local community, and a variety of proprietors selling food, religious items, and any number of possible gifts for the Christmas season. Saint Nicholas himself has made visits (looking suspiciously like Father Schierer).

A view of the St. Nicholas Market. *Amanda Bowman.*

The church façade also got a renovation. The three tympana (decorative stone arches) above the main doors of the church were planned but never carved when the church was built, and the 100th anniversary seemed the right time to enhance the façade of an already beautiful church. The tympanum project beautifies the blank space above the church building's front doors with sculpted images of our Lord, patroness St. Rita, and St. Thomas More, the patron saint of the diocese. The tympana above the side doors facing Russell Road have images of the Sacred Heart of Jesus and the Immaculate Heart of Mary. Underneath the center tympanum, the words *Christus Vincit, Christus Regnat, Christus Imperat* is carved ("Christ Conquers, Christ Reigns, Christ Commands"). Underneath the Sacred Heart is *Cor Iesu Misericors, Dona Nobis Pacem* ("Merciful Heart of Jesus, Grant Us Peace"), and underneath the Immaculate Heart, the words *Cor Mariae Dulcissimum, Iter Para Tutum* ("Most Sweet Heart of Mary, Prepare a Safe Path").

The designs for the tympana were developed in conjunction with Nic Charbonneau of Harrison Design. The images were refined and models created by Cody Swanson in Italy. The actual carving, which began in March 2024, was completed by Chris Pellettieri of New York. In addition to this project, other enhancements for the church were completed for the anniversary, including a new sound system installed in January 2024.

Top: Image for the tympanum project. *Father Christopher Christensen.*

Bottom: A three-dimensional image of the project. *Father Christopher Christensen.*

The school continues to develop. Normalcy has returned after the "COVID years." The classical model is being further implemented. In the church, the fate of the Traditional Latin Mass (as of spring 2024) at St. Rita remains uncertain given recent pronouncements. Regardless, the fathers at St. Rita remain committed to the faithful who are devoted to this Mass.

One of the biggest recent challenges has been the housing project that is being built next door to the parish and school. In late 2023, after much discussion, the old Safeway building next door was demolished, and a

Construction underway next to St. Rita. *Centennial History Subcommittee.*

A view of one of the faithful in prayer. *From the* Arlington Catholic Herald.

multi-year construction project that will eventually become a high-rise apartment complex began. Concerns about the safety and well-being of the schoolchildren during the building of the complex have been made known to the city, as well as concerns about access and parking for Mass and school.

Yet amid uncertainty, there is serenity and peace, as well as a further determination to evangelize and to spread the Gospel's good news. Father Christensen has made it a priority to do so in the local Chirilagua community, and he is looking for ways to promote family formation among the Spanish- and English-speaking communities.

Meanwhile, the parish and school thrive. There are more than 1,200 registered parish families and more than 3,500 registered parish members. School enrollment is at capacity with more than 250 students. Annually, there are many baptisms, First Communions, Confirmations, weddings, and funerals. Thousands of dollars and pounds of food are collected for the needy and hundreds of contacts made by parish groups to local residents, nursing homes, and to those in need of financial assistance. Thousands of hours have been volunteered among twenty-six parish groups and ministries. Sacramental grace is continuously provided. Hundreds of hours are spent in Eucharistic Adoration. Confessions are offered daily, and the lines are long. Multiple Masses are offered on Sundays in English, Latin, and Spanish, as well as twice-weekday Masses. At St. Rita, with God's grace, the impossible is indeed possible. What is certain, as St. Rita Parish moves into its next century of faith, is that the faithful will continue to continue to rely on the protection of their patroness, and continue to trust in the providence of God.

Appendix A

SISTERS OF ST. JOSEPH WHO SERVED AT ST. RITA SCHOOL, PARISH, AND CONVENT AND ST. RITA SCHOOL PRINCIPALS

SISTERS OF ST. JOSEPH WHO SERVED AT ST. RITA SCHOOL

Sister	Start Date	End Date	Ministry Title
Sister Marie Saint Paul Alspaugh	8/19/1978	8/15/1986	Principal
Sister Ave (Miriam Christi) Armstrong	8/21/1967	8/20/1971	Teacher
Sister Ave (Miriam Christi) Armstrong	8/21/1972	8/18/1978	Teacher
Sister Jeanne B. (Francis Lucille) Barnard	8/26/1965	8/18/1970	Teacher
Sister Genevieve Marie Beirne	8/21/1971	8/18/1975	Teacher
Sister Francis Genevieve Belz	8/21/1967	8/16/1968	Teacher
Sister Rose Margaret Brady	8/1/1971	7/31/1972	Teacher
Sister Catherine de Sales Braun	8/16/1968	8/12/1969	Teacher
Sister Regina Maria Brimmer	8/26/1952	8/15/1963	Teacher

Sister	Start Date	End Date	Ministry Title
Sister Audrey (Saint Madeleine) Butler	8/19/1970	9/4/1975	Teacher
Sister Ann Bernard Carlin	8/1/1972	7/31/1978	Principal
Sister Anna Mary Carr	8/1/1962	7/31/1964	Teacher
Sister Catherine Rosarii Cawley	8/1/1969	7/31/1972	Principal
Sister Agnes Leonore Condy	8/01/1965	7/31/1967	Teacher
Sister Rose Clare Coughlin	8/01/1952	8/27/1956	Teacher
Sister M. Jane (Mary Joanne) Coyle	8/01/1964	7/31/1970	Teacher
Sister Frances Amata (Francis Amata) Curran	7/01/1993	12/4/2008	School Secretary
Sister Thomas Regina Danks	8/01/1978	7/31/1983	Office Staff
Sister Marguerite Joseph Dawson	8/1/1953	8/31/1969	Teacher
Sister Marguerite Joseph Dawson	9/1/1969	7/31/1978	Office Staff
Sister Claire A. (Carmela) DeStefano	8/01/1961	7/31/1968	Teacher
Sister Evelyn (Andrew Michael) Dewey	8/01/1968	6/15/1970	Teacher
Sister Catherine Michael Fee	8/15/1991	8/31/1998	Principal
Sister Mary (Marian Edward) Fineran	8/01/1955	7/31/1959	Teacher
Sister Agnes Eileen Finley	8/1/1970	7/31/1971	Teacher
Sister Elizabeth Ann (Leonard Elizabeth) Fundalewicz	8/01/1977	7/31/1979	Teacher
Sister Alice (Joseph Therese) Gallagher	8/01/1960	7/31/1963	Teacher

Sister	Start Date	End Date	Ministry Title
Sister Saint Joan Gallagher	8/26/1952	8/20/1972	Teacher
Sister Helen Teresita Gerrity	8/01/1963	7/31/1966	Teacher
Sister Mary A. (Thomas Catherine) Gillespie	8/01/1978	7/31/1981	Teacher
Sister Saint Gervase Glackin	8/01/1969	7/31/1970	Teacher
Sister William Gerard Golden	8/1/1953	7/31/1957	Teacher
Sister William Gerard Golden	8/1/1983	1/9/1991	Office Staff
Sister Berenice C. (Denis Edward) Harp	8/1/1987	7/31/1988	Teacher
Sister Berenice C. (Denis Edward) Harp	8/1/1988	8/9/1990	Tutor
Sister Marie Saint William Harris	11/19/1961	8/24/1962	Teacher
Sister Michael Louis Hartman	8/17/1968	8/15/1969	Teacher
Sister Stella Immaculate Higgins	8/1/1971	7/31/1973	Teacher
Sister Alma Bernadette Hurley	7/01/2008	8/31/2018	School Volunteer
Sister Grace Fidelis Jannetti	8/23/1963	8/20/1967	Teacher
Sister Francis Elizabeth Keech	8/1/1971	7/31/1974	Teacher
Sister Maureen Patrick Kelly	8/10/1990	6/30/1995	Math/ Reading Teacher
Sister Marie Esther Kenny	8/1/1956	8/31/1961	Teacher
Sister Saint Dominic Knoll	8/16/1969	8/20/1971	Teacher
Sister Anne Benedict Kohl	8/22/1959	8/15/1969	Teacher

Sister	Start Date	End Date	Ministry Title
Sister Ann (Regina Veronica) Kramer	8/01/1967	7/31/1968	Teacher
Sister Loretta (Walburga) Krimm	8/1/1970	7/31/1971	Teacher
Sister Paul Anthony Kronberger	8/1/1959	7/31/1960	Teacher
Sister Jane E. (Paul Josepha) Lawrence	8/01/1972	7/31/1976	Teacher
Sister Jane E. (Paul Josepha) Lawrence	8/01/1986	8/14/1991	Principal
Sister Robert Vincent Lawrence	8/1/1974	7/31/1977	Teacher
Sister Cecilia Maria Leipert	8/01/1968	7/31/1972	Teacher
Sister Saint Robert Lipsett	8/11/1958	8/12/1964	Principal
Sister Mary Zita Logue	8/1/1954	7/31/1963	Teacher
Sister Francis Annice Lunney	8/01/2011	5/21/2018	Ministry Site Volunteer
Sister Eleanor Gertrude Mahony	8/16/1969	7/31/1973	Teacher
Sister Kathryn A. (David Catherine) Malone	8/01/1957	7/31/1960	Teacher
Sister Helen Gilbert Mann	8/01/1962	7/31/1965	Teacher
Sister Patricia (Joseph Kathleen) Martel	8/01/1977	7/31/1984	Teacher
Sister Theresa (Paul Christi) McCrossen	8/10/1990	8/14/1999	Teacher
Sister Theresa (Paul Christi) McCrossen	7/15/2004	6/30/2016	Teacher
Sister Theresa (Paul Christi) McCrossen	7/1/2016	6/30/2018	Resource Teacher
Sister Patricia Anne (Joan Kevin) McGarrity	8/01/1985	8/9/1990	Teacher

Sister	Start Date	End Date	Ministry Title
Sister Eileen T. (Thomas Magdalen) McGovern	8/01/1963	7/31/1965	Teacher
Sister Teresa M. (Saint Catherine) McKenna	8/01/1984	7/31/1987	Teacher
Sister Francis Patrick McMullan	8/19/1952	8/10/1958	Principal
Sister Francis Patrick McMullan	8/13/1964	8/15/1968	Principal
Sister Gertrude Louise Moloney	8/1/1955	7/31/1958	Teacher
Sister Joseph Eleanor Motzenbecker	8/01/1983	7/31/1985	School Secretary
Sister James Gabriel Mullin	8/25/1962	8/14/1964	Teacher
Sister Thomas Inez O'Neill	8/1/1960	7/31/1969	Teacher
Sister Saint Hubert O'Rourke	8/1/1958	10/31/1961	Teacher
Sister Marion A. (Adelina) Pfaff	8/1/1985	6/30/1993	Office Staff
Sister Edward Miriam Ryan	8/01/1978	7/31/1984	Teacher
Sister Louisa (Saint Oswald) Schumacher	8/01/1975	7/31/1978	Teacher
Sister Thomas Vincent Sheehan	8/1/1955	7/31/1961	Teacher
Sister Helen Gabriel Smith	8/01/1978	7/31/1985	Teacher
Sister Margaret Mary (Anne Cyrille) Smith	8/01/1957	7/31/1967	Teacher
Sister Rose Bernadette Snyder	8/01/1973	7/31/1977	Teacher
Sister Florence (Stanislaus) Sponga	8/01/1966	8/31/1966	Teacher
Sister Martin de Porres Stewart	9/10/1966	6/15/1968	Teacher

Sister	Start Date	End Date	Ministry Title
Sister Adele Marie Toal	8/1/1953	7/31/1955	Teacher
Sister Blanche Toomey	8/1/1952	7/31/1962	Teacher
Sister Phyllis Jewel (Philip Therese) Tracy	8/01/1976	7/31/1978	Teacher
Sister Mary Teresa (George Elizabeth) Willmanns	8/01/1963	7/31/1967	Teacher
Sister Emma M. (Andrew Catherine) Yondura	8/01/1988	8/14/1992	Teacher

SISTERS OF ST. JOSEPH WHO SERVED AT ST. RITA PARISH

Sister	Start Date	End Date	Ministry Title
Sister Teresa Immaculate Diamond	8/1/1970	7/31/1972	CCD Coordinator
Sister Catherine D. (Marie Josephine) Donohue	8/1/1972	7/31/1975	Director of Religious Education
Sister Marie Brigid Monaghan	8/01/1988	6/30/1993	Minister of Pastoral Care

SISTERS OF ST. JOSEPH WHO SERVED AT ST. RITA CONVENT (WORKSITE)

Sister	Start Date	End Date	Ministry Title
Sister Rose Margaret Brady	8/1/1972	7/31/1978	Resident
Sister Saint Joan Gallagher	8/21/1972	5/31/1979	Resident
Sister Alma Bernadette Hurley	9/1/2018	4/3/2019	Volunteer
Sister Mary Ida Post	8/1/1981	7/31/1987	Convent Helper

The following have served as St. Rita School principals since the school's founding in 1952:

Sister Francis Patrick McMullen	1952–58
Sister St. Robert Lipsett	1958–64
Sister Francis Patrick McMullan	1964–68
Sister Catherine Rosarii Cawley	1968–72
Sister Ann Bernard Carlin	1972–78
Sister Marie St. Paul Alspaugh	1978–86
Sister Jane Lawrence	1986–91
Sister Catherine Michael Fee	1991–98
Mrs. Mary P. Schlickenmaier	1998–2019
Mrs. Melissa M. Manaker	2019–20
Mrs. Bethany S. Hamm	2020–23
Mr. Maxwell F. Bindernagel	2023–24
Mrs. Malia C. Busekrus	2024–

A GUIDE TO ST. RITA CHURCH

A CATECHISM IN STONE AND GLASS

THE ARCHITECT SAMUEL COLLINS

The architect of St. Rita Church was Samuel Collins, a Catholic born in Washington, D.C., in 1881. His father was Thomas Jasper Collins, who was born in 1844 and served in the Union army before becoming an architect. In 1890, the elder Collins relocated his family to Staunton, Virginia, where he founded an architectural firm that became known as T.J. Collins and Sons when Samuel and his brother, William, joined the practice in 1906. The two brothers took over the firm completely when their father retired in 1911.

During its first two decades, the firm designed more than two hundred buildings in Staunton alone, many of which are now listed in the National Register of Historic Places. This rich architectural heritage spans diverse styles, ranging from Victorian and Italianate private homes to Neoclassical, Romanesque, and Beaux-Arts public buildings. The firm also built and restored numerous churches around the Commonwealth of Virginia and the Mid-Atlantic region. One example is St. Francis' Church in Staunton, which it restored in 1895. The firm also renovated St. Peter's Church in Harper's Ferry in the Gothic Revival style the following year.

After 1927, Samuel Collins left the family firm to work on his own. With this artistic freedom, he began to work on projects influenced by new developments in the Arts and Crafts movement, Art Nouveau, and modernism. He was also deeply versed in the rich history of Christian architecture, which is reflected in his adaptation of the Gothic style at

Above: Exterior of St. Paul Church in Richmond. *St. Paul Catholic Church, Richmond, Virginia*.

Left: Interior of St. Paul Church in Richmond. *St. Paul Catholic Church, Richmond, Virginia*.

St. Rita and at another church he built, St. Paul in Richmond. The two churches incorporate strikingly similar timber vaulting, plain limestone columns, and lance windows. But whereas the sanctuary of St. Paul has been heavily renovated over the years, and thus many of the original mosaics and other details forever lost, at St. Rita such details have been preserved almost entirely as they were when the church was completed some seventy-five years ago.

As his final achievement, Collins won the competition to design the Virginia War Memorial in Richmond. This modernist design on a truly

View looking from nave toward the sanctuary. *Joe Spalding.*

Aerial photo of Virginia War Memorial. *Virginia War Memorial Foundation.*

monumental scale is a stark departure from his earlier work. Unfortunately, he did not live to see it completed. He died in 1953 before construction of the War Memorial began in 1955. Fittingly, his funeral was held at St. Francis, which his father had designed.

The Church's Blend of Styles

In keeping with the Gothic Revival of the nineteenth and early twentieth centuries, the overall style of St. Rita Church is primarily Gothic, especially the exterior. St. Rita Church is laid out along the traditional east–west axis, which is filled with ancient significance, as even in pre-Christian pagan traditions, the east, where the sun rises, has always been associated with birth and life, whereas the west is associated with death. In the early Catholic Church, the rising sun began to be seen as a symbol of the risen Christ, who drives away the darkness of sin and death and who is Himself the light of the world. Thus, the rising sun illuminating the sanctuary in glorious rays of light during Sunday morning Mass is a sign of the light of Christ. When the priest celebrates Mass *ad orientem* (facing the altar, but literally meaning "toward the east") at St. Rita, he is truly looking to the east and also toward the coming of the Lord who will appear in clouds and majesty on the Last Day.

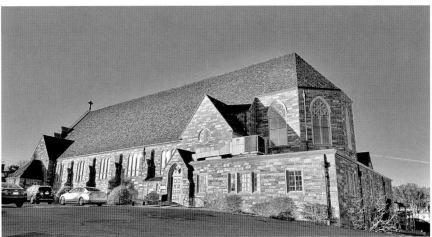

Top: Façade of St. Rita Church. *Dori Rutherford*.

Bottom: Looking at St. Rita Church from the southeast. *Joe Spalding*.

Within its overall Gothic Revival structure, the design of St. Rita incorporates elements from many eras that may escape first notice. On close look, one can see decorative details that include organic Art Nouveau motifs in the capitals of the columns in the nave, Arts and Crafts tiles and ironwork in the altar rail (as well as the baptistery), and even certain near-modernist mosaics on the altars. The proportions of the columns suggest an Art Deco influence inspired by Egyptian forms. The wood paneling of the pulpit and organ loft suggest the Tudor period, as does the mullioned stained glass of the lance windows and the narthex screen. There are architectural and other touches inspired by early Norman churches. This eclectic merging of styles does not detract from the overall appearance but instead makes St. Rita seem older than it really is—as medieval churches themselves often contain a variety of different styles and renovations that accrued over the centuries.

Entering through the Portal into the Narthex

Entering through one of the three portals via the main west entrance, one sees just above each of the three doors a semicircular wall surface (tympanum). Cost reductions when the church was built left the tympana unfinished, although these were recently completed for the parish's 100th anniversary. The narthex (or vestibule) within is not only a place of entrance into St. Rita Church, but it is also the place of entrance into *the* Universal Church as the location of the baptistery, which also echoes the common English practice of having a side porch for the primary entrance. The narthex is also the portal through which the faithful go forth, glorifying the Lord by their lives, and the beginning and ending of Eucharistic processions that bring Christ to the world. Within the narthex, Our Lady of Guadalupe is depicted as a reminder both of the vibrancy of the Spanish-speaking community at St. Rita and of Our Lady's patronage of the Americas. A statue of Our Lady of Guadalupe also stands in the close (or courtyard) in front of the rectory.

St. Rita does not have a bell tower, similar to early Norman churches, but it does have a great window above the organ loft, reminiscent of the later perpendicular Gothic style. Although difficult to see from the ground, the great window depicts symbols of the four evangelists flanking a gate or tower, suggestive of the New Jerusalem and the narrow gate through which only the righteous will enter. The gate also has a monogram of Our Lady, reminding us that the church is walking with Peter, to Jesus, through Mary.

Left: Wrought-iron gates leading to the baptistery. *Joe Spalding.*

Below: Statue of Our Lady of Guadalupe. *Joe Spalding.*

Choir loft and organ. *Joe Spalding.*

THE NAVE

Entering into the nave, one sees that the floor plan is a traditional Latin cross, with side aisles common to many medieval churches, although compressed to the humbler proportions of an ordinary parish church. The interior of the church, while not stark or cold, is simple. This is not dissimilar to medieval churches found in England or France, but it also was a practical decision. While building the church, Samuel Collins complained in a letter to Bishop Ireton that construction costs had doubled during the postwar building boom. The original Neoclassical brick church for St. Ann Parish in Arlington was completed in 1947 and was significantly over budget. Cost-saving measures proposed for St. Rita included using brick instead of stone for the exterior and eliminating the narthex. Fortunately, these changes were not necessary. Leaving the ceiling panels exposed instead of being plastered was a result of economizing, and the original plan for an undercroft (basement) also had to be scaled back to a storage area under the sanctuary only.

This minimalism of embellishment is reminiscent of early English Norman churches but also points to a more near-modernist adaptation of the Gothic style. This is especially evident in the clean lines of the stonework. Medieval churches in Europe are filled with ornamentation and decoration on practically every surface. In the Middle Ages, they were also places of constant activity. For illiterate peasants, churches were "visual Bibles" and perhaps the only place they would see fine art in their whole lives. Conversely, for a distracted modern age, the sparseness of St. Rita provides an oasis of calm and reflection.

The nave of a church takes its name from the nautical appearance of the timbers that form the roof. The exposed framing makes this particularly noticeable at St. Rita. Looking upward, it is easy to imagine the entire church as an inverted ship, with the ribs and keel forming the ceiling. Indeed, in medieval times, shipbuilders were often employed in the construction of

Original St. Ann Church in 1949. *St. Ann Catholic Church, Arlington, Virginia.*

Left: Statue of the Infant of Prague. *Joe Spalding*

Right: Statue of St. Anthony of Padua. *Joe Spalding*

churches. There are also many examples of churches laid out with the same proportions that were given to Noah for the construction of the ark. This rich symbolism is reinforced further in the set of nave windows that show the Barque of Peter and the anchor, both of which recall the crossing of the Sea of Galilee and the struggles of the faithful in the world.

At the rear of the nave are statues of the Infant of Prague and St. Anthony with the Infant Jesus, both reminders that our Lord came to us as a helpless baby sharing fully in our human nature in everything but sin, and which make a connection between the Church and Our Lady's womb. Mary is the mother of the Church and the preeminent member of the Church, so reminders of her presence are fitting. The images of the Christ Child are juxtaposed with the gilded carvings of the Stations of the Cross, which depict the events of the Lord's Passion. This venerable devotion assists the faithful in calling to mind that just as our Lord came into the world according to the flesh to suffer and to die, the faithful are also called to take up our crosses and follow him.

Other windows in the nave contain images pertaining to the mission of the Church. The three fishes and the Lamb of God promise the reward of the heavenly banquet for those who keep the faith and the Lord's commandments. The scepter and crown and the phoenix symbolize the rebirth and kingship of the people of God in our baptism. The descending dove and the New Testament with the Cross and Crown of Thorns illustrate the graces of the Holy Spirit and the nourishment of the scriptures that sustain us in our pilgrim way. Meanwhile, the symbols on the pews of various floral motifs call to mind the lilies of the field as a reminder of divine providence in the ordinary lives of the people of God.

The Transept and Sanctuary

Toward the front of the nave, above the confessionals on either side, is found a final pair of windows that depict the divine hand of God at creation on the right and the flaming sword and scales of the Last Judgment on the left. These windows remind the faithful that God is the eternal alpha and omega (beginning and end) who we will come to see face to face at the end of time. The transept (crossing)—the point at which nave and sanctuary meet—is truly the crossing point into the eternal realm. The side aisles each lead to a smaller altar with Joseph and Christ the King to the right and Mary, under the title Seat of Wisdom with the infant Jesus, and St. Rita the church's patroness, to the left. Approaching the sanctuary from any direction, the visitor's eye is always drawn toward the eternal.

The Arts and Crafts tiles below the altar rail (between the nave and sanctuary) are also a blend of ancient and modern. Similar tiles also lined the steps that led up to the high altar before it was renovated in the 1960s. All these tiles were manufactured by hand at the Moravian Pottery and Tile Works of Doylestown, Pennsylvania. The works were founded in 1911 by Henry Chapman Mercer, an eccentric character and something of a

Clockwise from top left: St. Joseph's Altar. Statue of Christ the King. Statue of St. Rita. Mary's Altar. *Centennial History Subcommittee.*

Mary's Altar is also used as the Altar of Repose on Holy Thursday. *Joe Spalding.*

Detail of mosaic in Mary's Altar. *Peter Church.*

Composite of Mercer tiles. *Peter Church.*

Renaissance man. Independently wealthy, he traveled the world studying ancient techniques that he painstakingly reproduced with modern methods, and these tiles were one of his greatest achievements and also earned him great renown within the Arts and Crafts movement. Mercer modeled his patterns after tiles rescued from the Castle Acre Priory after the destruction of the monasteries by Henry VIII and held in the collections of the British Museum, as well as other designs he found in the course of his travels through Europe and Asia.

Like the other decorative elements, the tiles are a small detail that can easily be missed without careful observation. Each detail is the work of artisans whose stories are too numerous and lengthy to recount in full here, and the expense of this craftsmanship was funded through the sacrificial gifts of parish families. Each carving and each window is an expression of many talents united toward a common purpose, just as the Universal Church joins many in one body, contributing in untold ways both seen and unseen for the greater glory of God.

In the sanctuary itself are five stained-glass windows. Two depict symbols of Christ's passion such as His wounds and the implements of the Crucifixion. Two more depict the sacrifices of the Old Testament and the Eucharistic sacrifice of the New Testament. The central window shows the Holy Spirit descending with His gifts and the pelican, a symbol of Christ feeding His people with His blood. Each of these five windows is topped with a rose window, having eight rays, which conveys deep and transcendent symbolism about the fullness of time in God's plan for salvation and which is prefigured in the eight days of Jewish celebrations such as Hanukkah. Likewise, the octaves of the liturgical calendar mark Sunday—the day of the Resurrection—as the final day of creation, which stands outside of time but also completes it. Two more rose windows, one on each end of the transept, bring the total number of rose windows to seven—the days of the earthly week, reinforcing the symbolism at this junction between the temporal and the eternal.

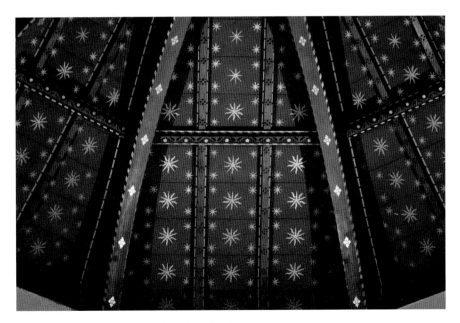

Detail of stars on sanctuary ceiling. *Peter Church.*

Looking toward the main altar. *Joe Spalding*.

The sanctuary itself is physically elevated above the rest of the church as a fitting setting for the Holy Sacrifice of the Mass, which is the source and summit of the Catholic faith. The arched ceiling depicts the stars of the heavens, recalling creation and the harmony with which God made the universe, a harmony only restored by Christ's sacrifice. Behind the tabernacle where the Blessed Sacrament perpetually resides, the reredos contains an abstract pattern that evokes Christ, the True Vine to which the faithful are grafted as members of the Body of Christ. Ministering angels hover above the crucifix and tabernacle, where the veil between the temporal and eternal is torn asunder. The inscription on the altar is *INRI NIKA. INRI* is the inscription that was placed on the cross above Jesus and means "Jesus of Nazareth, King of the Jews." *NIKA* is the Greek verb meaning "conquer." Thus, Jesus of Nazareth, King of the Jews, conquers. It is here during the Holy Sacrifice of the Mass that the Crucifixion, Christ's ultimate victory over sin and death, is made present over and over again in an unbloody form. Truly, He is victorious!

ACKNOWLEDGEMENTS

The St. Rita Centennial History Book Subcommittee has many to thank in the preparation of this history of our parish. Over the course of nearly a year, we have benefited from their prayers, good will, and resources. Of course, first and foremost, *Ad Majorem Dei Gloriam*! It is through God that all good things come. We thank our spiritual leaders: Bishop Michael Burbidge for his guidance and his foreword to this history; our pastors and priests, past and present, for their direction, and in particular our current pastor, Father Christopher Christensen, who approved this project and its funding; and our parochial vicar, Father Nicholas Schierer. We also especially thank our parish's permanent deacon, Deacon Stephen Dixon, who has led the centennial project and has been a steady source of guidance and inspiration as well.

We have interviewed and obtained information from many during this journey, and we include in our thanks the following: Lindsay Alukonis (for her help with the Diocese of Arlington archives), Susanne Arnold, Nicholas Barrows, Debbie Beck, Max Bindernagel, Lawrence Bowie, Amanda Bowman, Dan Cotter (from the Mother of Light Center), Josephine Cunningham, Leigha and Paul Doerrer, Maria Patricia Downey, Chris Durel, Ryan Ellis, Mike Fenwick, Elizabeth Fitton, Eamonn Greiner, Kitty Guy and Virginia Nyce (for help with the Basilica of St. Mary archives), Bethany Hamm, Chris and Cindy Hart, Gary Hermann, Edie Jeter (from the Diocese of Richmond), Kelly McArtor, Nancy McKeague, Ann McLaughlin, Katherine Quan (for the 100th anniversary logo), Alma

Ramirez, Dori Rutherford, Kevin Schweers (and others from the *Arlington Catholic Herald*), Maureen Schweers, Mary Pat Schlickenmaier, Paul Skevington, Joe Spalding, and Elizabeth Vail.

We likewise thank Father Denis Donahue, Father Andrew Fisher, Father Daniel Gee, Father Mark Moretti, Father Robert Rippy, and Father Paul Scalia among the clergy, as well as Sister Alma Bernadette Hurley, SSJ, and Sister Theresa McCrossen, SSJ, among the religious sisters.

We have referred to many sources in researching and writing this history. Articles that we found in the *Arlington Catholic Herald* and the *Catholic Virginian* were of great assistance. Research in our own St. Rita Parish archives, as well as the archives of the Dioceses of Arlington and Richmond and in the Office of Historic Alexandria, bore great fruit. Thanks to all who assisted us who work at those locations. The Sisters of St. Joseph provided the list of Sisters who faithfully served at St. Rita, and we have used that list in Appendix A. In 1974, for the fiftieth anniversary, the parish published a locally printed history of St. Rita that we have relied on greatly for this project. We thank the men and women who worked on that fine history—it has been an invaluable resource for us.

We thank Rick and Soraya Strobach for their Spanish translation of a special part of this history. And we also thank Kate Jenkins at The History Press, who has been our stalwart supporter throughout the entire process, and Ryan Finn, senior editor at The History Press, for his guidance as well.

Finally, we thank all the faithful at St. Rita Parish, at both school and church, over the past one hundred years and more, for their unwavering faith and commitment. And as always, we thank our patroness, St. Rita of Cascia. Our patron saint of impossible causes has shown us throughout the years that with God's grace, all things are indeed possible.

ABOUT THE CONTRIBUTORS

The research, writing, and editing of this book was the work of members of the St. Rita History Book Subcommittee, part of the St. Rita Centennial Committee, which was chaired by Deacon Stephen Dixon. The members of the subcommittee included Joshua Bowman, Danny Ciatti, Sarah Greiner, Walt Hudson, and David Sullivan.